# Fred

# Fred:
*An unbecoming woman*

## Annie Krabbenschmidt

Radical Queer Dinner Party Books
*Los Angeles, 2022*

RQDP Books
radicalqueerdinnerparty.com

Copyright © Annie Krabbenschmidt 2022

Drawings by Anna Alcaro (the good ones) and Annie Krabbenschmidt (the less good ones)
Pictures provided by Dawn O'Dell
Cover & Interior Designed & Typeset by Colleen Sheehan
RQDP logo designed by Marie Corriveau

ISBN: 979-8-9850432-0-4

This is a book of memoir and non-fiction. All events are described as I remember them, which is not to say that my memory is any more accurate than anyone else's; to the best of my ability, this is a completely true account of events, but much of the mind is mysterious and self-centered, and therefore I accept that some events may not have happened *exactly* as I remember. But I'm not about to try to undermine a democratic election and create a dumb website called truth.com, because I'm not an autocrat.

*For my dad, who gave me my head,
my mom, who gave me my heart,
and my sister, who gave me my humility.*

*The pursuit of individual happiness does not trump or excuse our obligations to each another. We are in this together, this accumulation of scars, this world of objects, this physical and temporary heaven that so often takes on the countenance of hell. What matters is kindness; what matters is solidarity. What matters is staying alert, staying open, because if we know anything from what has gone before us, it is that the time for feeling will not last.*

*Olivia Laing, The Lonely City*

# Appendix I:
# Enjoying This Book

FIRST CF ALL, I hope that you do enjoy it ! Though I've already managed to stuff this book with far more words, drawings, and pictures than is reasonable, there's more! Throughout this book there are several QR codes that link to songs or videos. To scan a QR code, just open your phone's camera app, point it at the pixels, and follow the link. You may need to tap on the image to help bring it into focus!

You can practice on the following QR code, which will direct you to a collection of playlists that accompany select chapters throughout this book.

# Appendix II: Timeline of Events

Kiss Paige — Annie Broken leg — Stephanie — My first suit — YOU, HERE, NOW!

xy

Curse on Paige and her entire family

Move to New York

lift curse

Katie

Julie has the gall to suggest I haven't accepted my sexuality

I acknowledge that I may not have accepted my sexuality

# Contents

| | |
|---|---|
| Introduction | 1 |
| An Absolutely Shocking Twist | 7 |
| Coming Out | 15 |
| Coming Out in Love | 32 |
| Coming Out of Love | 45 |
| Concerning Hobbits and Vibrators | 64 |
| Intermission | 86 |
| Coming Out ... Again | 116 |
| Half Windsors and Best Men | 117 |
| Coming Out ... Again? | 135 |
| ITC | 136 |
| Still ... Coming Out | 154 |
| Lovers and Friends | 155 |
| Oh, I Get it, You Never Stop Coming Out | 173 |
| Apple Cider Donuts | 175 |
| Okay, I'm Done Here | 189 |
| Introvert's Burlesque | 190 |
| Epilogue | 212 |

# Introduction

I'M NOT CONVINCED that I deserve your attention. You may shut this book right now, remembering that you meant to finally start watching *Mare of Easttown*. But it would be terrible to let your decisions, and your objectively good decision-making skills, influence mine. So with or without you, I've written this book.

On a bone-chilling New York night, I crammed myself, and a down jacket the size of a small child, into the back tavern of a Long Island City bar. Among others, Leslie Jamison read from an essay and signed books. She wrote in my copy of *The Empathy Exams*: "For Annie—Here's to empathy in all its futility and possibility." And that's right, isn't it?

Nothing truly matters, at least not in the cosmic sense. If I were to wait for the conviction that my art would matter in that way—become a distinguishable fold in the fabric of humanity—I would have been waiting for my entire insignificant lifetime. But of course, my story, my odyssey, my saga, my *There and Back Again*, is everything that I am, is the very thing that makes me a human. My idiosyncrasies and oddities weave a complex maze of a portrait of *me*, the young woman, Ann; making my way to the heart of the matter is the singular mission of my life as a writer.

In a graduate school seminar, a psychology professor stated that scientists have no clear definition of the self. Here's what I know to be obvious: that exploring the self is the work of artists, and those attempting to define it while working in the world of certainty will likely never achieve it.

I think I had conviction once. Back when I was also an asshole. I had the brazen confidence to pose as indomitable without seeing that I was actually wound so tightly (and wounded so deeply) that the risk of springing undone was getting greater by the second. Back then, I probably could have written an entire book in one sitting, believing I was right about everything I thought. When, as a child, I made fun of sensitive people for being "crybabies," I never imagined that I would become someone in a corporate office, weeping at my desk, wondering why I just couldn't quite make my life work.

But, being sheltered, I was so wrong about so many things. And when I learned just how wrong I could be, as I peeled away layers of my ignorance, I feared so much the thoughtless things I might say. Then came the added hurdle that some people would tell me I was wrong, even if I was right. [See also *gaslighting* and *structural misogyny*].

For many years, the fear of being wrong, or being made to feel a fool, stopped me from writing. This was not as much a function of humility as it was a desperate hope to remain perfect. In my world—the Marin County, nuclear-American-family, Lululemon-wearing, Duke University world—the unblemished are revered.

But again, certainty and cleanliness are antithetical to writing, which asks that you say something new and therefore brave. Writer's block is, most often, not an inability to put pen to paper (anyone can force themselves to describe their breakfast in words), but a frustrating state in which you can't stop picturing the judgmental reader, wondering if what you say matters at all. This nagging perfectionism, the inner voice that tells you to stop writing, is a call to safety.

James Baldwin wrote in *The Fire Next Time*, that "to act is to be committed, and to be committed is to be in danger." Writing is an act of danger, and it's understandable to say that queer people have already had our fair share of it. We walk on a balance beam, carrying the weight of our identities, worried that we might just prove the world right—maybe we are as backwards and screwed up as people say.

But facing this danger is how we grow. So I hope you'll picture me, well aware of my foolishness as I humbly take shots in the dark, hoping my arrows spell something close to meaning.

A former friend once spotted me writing in my notebook and asked—the way you might ask a toddler who has just shown you a page full of misspelled words—"Are you writing in your diary?" I felt ashamed, as if there was something naïve about documenting my life. The fact that young girls are mocked for pouring their hearts out while Alexander Hamilton has a whole play written about his need to scribble is a structural deterrent for many people whose stories we most need to hear. Writers write. That's what we do when we put pen to paper. Maybe we should spend less time making fun of a document that starts "Dear diary" and start wondering why a diary is the only entity some people feel worthy of addressing. Women's writing is frivolous because we have decided that women are frivolous; the danger of commitment looms large for someone who risks frivolity, foolishness even, and decides to speak anyway.

I stand by every word I've written in this book. I have thought long and hard about what I wanted to say, why, and how. This project started with a question: "Why was it so hard to come out of the closet?" It is an important question, one that all of us should desperately want the answer to—to ask why it is that for some, we can more easily picture killing ourselves than living full and happy lives. Halfway through writing, I realized that the real question I was asking is, "What does it take to feel free? To forget the closet altogether?"

But to dismantle the closet is to call into question the structural integrity of the house in which that closet sits, not as an act of revenge but as an act of shared healing. This is an inquiry free of vengefulness.

I would imagine that, at times, I've come off as overly critical. I fear that the people that will have to bear the biggest burden of this critique are the people who least deserve it—and in fact deserve all the gratitude that I can offer.

My parents are superlative in all ways. Everything I am is because of them; everything in this book is because of them. They are there in every turn of phrase and in its very existence. My personhood—the extensive, well-documented list of my goddess-like qualities—are gifts that they have given me. I am sure it will feel as though I have made it my mission to pick at their tiniest faults, but I'm less concerned with blaming my parents for the choices they made than I am in understanding the world that made those choices the obvious ones. I fear that I have written a book that attacks the very moon and stars that have guided their world.

Yet, I must write this book, and I must write it in this way. I must because many of my documented experiences are relatable for much of my queer community. For many of us, the strain on our lives is not the overt homophobia of a few mean-spirited people but rather the disregard and lack of empathy en masse. A system of power does not persist due to the strategic actions of cruel people; it persists because well-intentioned people don't realize that they are guarding the gates to our freedom. Tiny acts of violence occur because they belong so seamlessly in a world that *seems* logical, free, and fair.

This book is far more optimistic than it may initially appear. Like most activists, I am deeply hopeful that people will try to do good if they know how.

And I swear, I tried not to write, to be more useful instead.

My senior year of college, my close friend and mentor asked me, "If you don't want to write, why do you carry a notebook?"

I shrugged and told him that I used to harbor the selfish dream of writing comedy, like Tina Fey. I told him—proudly, I guess—that I had learned my lesson, that writing was self-indulgent.

"It's all self-indulgent," he said with Obi-Wan fingers.

I just didn't know that what I wanted was important simply because I wanted it.

How do I know that my stories are important enough to write down? Because I, for one, couldn't stop telling them.

And this recounting promises to be as meaningful as any other account of human life, which is to say both infinitely and negligibly so. This book has been the very air that I breathe—it has both filled me up in my entirety and, as exhalation, has been removed from me forever, no more a part of me than footprints I've left in a well-vacuumed carpet.

But it just so happens that words, and the vulnerability that honest words bring, are how I offer myself to the world—how I tell my friends and the eight or so people who listen to the podcast I cohost that they are not alone, that the world can be safe sometimes. Or, I should say, more realistically, that safety at the expense of authenticity is a silent death.

That honesty is worth the pain that might come along with it.

That the grotesque viscera of our souls are miraculous entanglements, important to examine and stunning to witness.

# An Absolutely Shocking Twist

GROWING UP, I knew that when I turned sixteen, I would be madly in love. I would have had a boyfriend sooner, but there was one logistical issue: my parents told me I couldn't date before I was sixteen. But I knew that once I crossed that threshold, everyone around me would realize that I was girlfriend material. I spent the first two years of high school feeling guilty about the fact that I would have to break the heart of any gentleman to come my way, citing strict parents. "But!" I would say, "If you wait for me, I'm sure they will shower you with riches and splendor and more because you endured the absolute agony of having to go without me for a single second."

Often, I pondered this: the agony that those boys were facing; the thought of telling someone that I could not date him and make him the happiest man in the world. It was much too much for me to bear. So I avoided men as best I could.

I mean, I couldn't help but flirt, just a little, because I wanted them to know that, emotionally, I was interested. For example, there was one boy in my math class, Eddy, with whom I would have friendly competitions about quiz and test scores. I'd flash him my perfect results and give him a sexy eye roll when he did the same. I would playfully scoff at homework solutions and offer my services as a tutor, which would be a convenient way to show off my intelligence in a private setting. Of course, after class I would dash away before any solidified plans could be made. I wouldn't want the temptation to be too overwhelming.

So that's how I had to play it. Hot and cold. And I was an excellent flirt. One second it was, "Hey, do you want me to teach you how to actually *throw* a football?" and the next it was, "Sorry, I'd rather play with someone who knows how to hit his mark on the snap." It was the perfect balance to keep them interested from afar.

Now, on the eve of my sixteenth year, there was only one thing on my mind: my perfect future boyfriend. He would be tall, to help me reach things; probably blond, to complement my darker features; slender, to offset my softer belly. He would be funny and boisterous but also intelligent and sensitive. He would tell me about his insecurities and delicately brush my hair out of my eyes. He would tell me how beautiful I was when I cried and wipe my snot away with his hands, which would be soft and tender, but also calloused from lifting my body weight at the gym. He would be secure in his faults, humble. He would challenge me to be better and smarter but somehow convince me that I was already perfect.

I didn't think it was too much to ask of the universe to just provide me with the one person who fit into all these categories. Sure, the odds were stacked against me: my class only had thirty boys in it. I didn't need to be a mathlete (which I was, as I often reminded Eddy) to know that my odds were not good. But despite the slim pickings—the boys that were wee enough to be lifted up onto the shoulders of other boys—and those of some girls, too—I considered every contender with an open mind. The possibility of depth was lurking around every corner, and no matter how many viewings of *Donnie Darko* I had to sit through, I was going to find it.

I'll admit, I was a little surprised when people didn't come running when I finally turned sixteen. But I'm sure people were dealing with a lot of feelings. They had held back for so long and now they were finally free to love me. Sometimes unrestrained freedom can lead to confusion. Like when you live on your own for the first time and want to have ice cream for three meals a day. I was like the cappuccino choco-chip of those endless ice cream bowls—I'd keep you awake at night, and I was slightly exotic (assuming one quarter Italian qualifies for your definition of exotic). Soon, someone would be bound to lose his sense of control and sweep me off my feet. They would recover from the years of being brushed off by me. They would try again. So I waited.

I quickly realized that I would not make any progress with the popular boys in my class. Why? Well, if agreeing to watch

*Donnie Darko* again and getting my mom to drive fifteen minutes out of her way to make sure they got home from parties weren't successful strategies, then what could be done? They were unintelligent Cro-Magnons, and my assessment of a human was clearly on a different scale from those that determined high school popularity. I had a discerning eye. I had high standards. Why would I date someone *everyone* wanted?

When I found myself losing patience, I looked to role models for reassurance. Hermione Granger, for example. An exemplary student, it took seven years for her to get her nose out of her books long enough to finally kiss Ron. The best kinds of love are the ones that hit you when you least expect it, like when Hermione almost died stabbing a Horcrux with a basilisk fang before kissing Ron. Maybe I wouldn't find him at the first party I went to. In fact, the more parties I attended without finding my soulmate, the more it would mean to turn around in slow motion and stare directly into the eyes of my one true love with my hair blowing behind me.

Little did I know, the fateful moment wouldn't be at a party, but somewhere I least expected to find love: a Model UN conference.

I was representing Chile. With a stack of national briefs and a plan to form a southwestern-South American transnational alliance, an unprofessional affair between delegates was the last thing on my mind. In walked my fellow Chilean representative. Aiden. I'd known him for two years, but suddenly the way he charmed his way through international deals with light political banter made me look twice. We would walk around the conference telling people that due to our recent earthquake, Chile was on "shaky ground" and then run away, snickering at our audacity! We had so much fun with our gag that we didn't enter a single caucus, distracted by our attempt to meet every nation's delegate. Never have I let myself be so overcome with personal matters as to completely neglect the needs of my country. For this weekend only, I was grateful that my actions at Model UN had no real impact on national infrastructure.

After the conference, we texted every day for a week, recalling our days as Chilean ambassadors. We'd pass each other at school and say "CHILE," a sure sign that he treasured this weekend as much as I did. We didn't need to have longer conversations because the one word really said it all.

At the end of the week, we both ended up at a party. I knew I had to make my move. Well, I had to force myself to make my move. I pounded a couple of root beers and approached him. We stood in a corner of the room talking. Then he said, "Do you want to go outside?" So we did. We were sitting on a staircase and getting really close, but still, nothing happened. So he said, "Do you want to go over to that trampoline?" So we did. But still nothing happened. Then my friend called and said we had to go. So then he said, "Do you want to do this?" And we did. By which I mean I clenched my eyes shut and he kissed me. By which I mean he slobbered on the side of my face. I said I had to go, "but text me!" I ran back to my friend, and we talked excitedly about my clandestine love story. He did text me, immediately after. He wrote, "Chile!"

Oh, I smiled and squealed. But on the inside, I couldn't help but be a little disappointed. Was it just me, or did he try way too hard to be funny? I mean how many times was he going to make that Chile joke? I knew it wouldn't last, but of course, because of a slight communication error on my part, we were "together" for two arduous months and only had one vertical make-out session. We went on one date. He made me drive myself; was chivalry dead? Then he had the audacity to pay for my pizza; what, was he trying to be chivalrous? There was clearly something off about this kid. I would have broken it off sooner, but I somehow never saw him face to face again. We agreed to meet up to talk about what was going on, why I was no longer showing up to Model UN meetings, but the idea of looking him in the face and disappointing him was just too disheartening. For his own sake, I called him to break things off.

What was happening to me? Had my parents' prepubescent ban on men affected my libido? Would I forever find them to be mere opponents in my quest to get the highest test scores in my AP Calculus class? Or was I just destined to wait for the more mature and sophisticated men that college had to offer. I wasn't desperate, I was just faced with suboptimal choices.

By the time I was a senior, I was bound for Duke University, an institution known for churning out *only* decent men. I assured myself, "Your time will come. Be patient."

When I arrived at Duke, I was no longer patient and I was certainly desperate. I had graduated high school at the top of my game—captain of two sports teams, class president, generally liked by underclassmen, and I had eventually triumphed over Eddy when I ended up in a more advanced senior math class than he did. I had outgrown those thirty boys, and now no one was more deserving of a man than I was. ME.

I was on the hunt.

The first party I went to was hosted by a frat and freshmen girls were absolute royalty. I'm sure I would have stood out even if I hadn't worn my most stylish striped cardigan. How many of these freshman girls had *curricula vitae* that rivaled mine?[1]

I walked into a room full of tall, smart, fun, perfect, sophisticated, and mature men. Sweaty and dry humping each other and anyone that came in the room. They were mine for the taking, especially if I were to undo the top button on my sweater. Out of the corner of my eye, I saw one of them walking toward me: medium height, well-styled hair, two solo cups in hand, eyes glowing green, blue, and now red from the nearby disco light. He held one cup out to me. As my fingers brushed against his and I waited for the spark of a long-awaited destiny, I realized that there was just one logistical issue: at that exact moment, I knew for the first time that I was unquestionably, 100% gay.

Me. A gay. How?

Dropping my cup into the abyss of the frat house floor, I fled the scene with tears welling in my eyes. I took the next campus bus back to my freshman dorm. While others were just beginning their nights, their *lives*, I was seeing mine—at least in the way that I had known it—end. I stared out the window, hoping

---

[1] Oh, all of them? Okay, cool.

to catch a glimpse of the dark depth of my own despair, but instead all I saw was my own fluorescent reflection.

There had never been any logistical issues. Only one fundamental issue. And while I used to like that my life resembled one long episode of *30 Rock*, the best show for a girl aspiring to find loneliness amusing, I realized that I was no Liz Lemon after all. I wouldn't be getting my happy ending with a hot dog chef. What was there to look forward to if not wieners?

# Coming Out

THE KNOWLEDGE THAT I was—and had always been—a homosexual destroyed almost everything I knew about myself. For about a week, my stomach turned inside out; my body twisted all over itself in an effort to purge myself of this truth—to say nothing of the fear I had for the future. If I wasn't the shrewd heterosexual that I had thought I was, then I really didn't know the first thing about myself.

I wasn't concerned that someone might find out. For one thing, my libido was petrified, so no one was going to catch me in the *act* of gayness. For another, I was alarmingly good at fulfilling others' expectations; I could chameleon myself right into straightness, as I had done for the previous eighteen years.

What really scared me was that, in order to feel like I was being authentic, I would have to tell people something quite important about myself. In high school, I'd had so much holding up my identity—the sports that grounded me, the teachers that supported me, and my family who, even on our worst days, shared a house with me. Stripped of everything, I was suddenly hyperaware of this secret of mine and every other secret I'd ever had. I had been lied to, at my very own hand, and now I didn't know what was true about me and what was performance.

At first, I felt a sense of urgency to come out. I wrote a letter to my older sister, who was a senior at Penn, and choreographed the physical humor that would accompany it. I would deliver the letter to her personally then hide in her closet. The end of the letter would read, "Read this part out loud: 'You can go ahead and come out of the closet now.'" And then I would, well, come out of the closet. Maybe sobbing, maybe with jazz hands, maybe (likely) both. That kind of humor feels fresh when you've been sitting on your potential to make gay jokes for eighteen years.

Me? Drama? Yes, I know her well. When I was nine, I had a piano instructor named Dr. Ira, whom I convinced to abandon instruction and simply play show tunes for an hour. I would lean on my parents' black baby grand piano, serenading the empty living room. That's how I learned to spell O-K-L-A-H-O-M-A.

As an eighteen-year-old in DOMA[2]-era America, coming out felt like it needed that kind of showmanship. I abandoned my plan to write Catherine a letter—only because I thought I would need a major movie release instead. I mean that quite literally. Alone in my dorm room, or sometimes sobbing in the hall shower, I storyboarded an actual feature film about a sus-

---

[2] The Defense of Marriage Act, instated in 1996 by President Bill Clinton and struck down 2013, allowed states to make same-sex marriage illegal. Mine is the last generation that experienced its coming of age when same-sex marriage was not nationally recognized. Hopefully.

piciously Annie-like character who lives as a worried, closeted gay youth.[3] There would be an epigraph for the film, apologizing to my family and loved ones.

For what?

Apologizing felt so inherent to coming out. I had so much guilt and so much shame, like I had let people down. I was baptized Roman Catholic by way of my Italian family, but I was never a believer. I was, however, a devout Capitalist, and I was having a crisis of faith. I had done everything right: I got good grades, I captained my teams, I served as class president three years out of four.[4] I fulfilled my familial duties by going to a top-ten university in order to eventually attain a job that paid at least three billion dollars a year. I had reached the pinnacle of success.

I. Did. It.

So why was I being punished with this fate that would make my life more difficult when I had been promised, if I took all the right steps in childhood, that it would be easy.

• X • X • X •

I spent a lot of time alone that semester. The good friends I eventually made in college would describe the version of me from this period as "mute Annie," due to my uncharacteristic reservedness in comparison to the version of me they grew

---

[3] This was years before *Love, Simon* came out, but I swear to gourd that screenplay could have been ripped from my college journal.

[4] My junior year, I lost to Sarah Lee, who ran on the campaign that "nobody doesn't like Sarah Lee." Sarah Lee, you adorable mastermind.

to know—the version that routinely sang "Defying Gravity" en route to away games. And by that point, I didn't even mind singing alone; it allowed me to really show off my vibrato. The point of my Broadway braggery here is to demonstrate that I'm someone who is constantly making noise. Another perfectly valid example would be when a fourth-grade language arts teacher once counted how many times I talked in a group discussion about a book, and then pointed out in front of the whole class that this was considered too much.[5] All to say, being a quiet Annie felt very wrong; but I worried that people would hear the fear of a closeted lesbian in my voice.

In the first month of school, I would walk out of a Thursday-night physics recitation and walk past the Duke chapel, which was lit from below in a most sinister manner. I would crane my neck, looking for answers—or rather, I would mime all the postures a good Catholic would assume when looking for answers. Surely a merciful god would transcend my heathenness to guide me to salvation. Surely a merciful god would want that for me, instead of letting me wonder, night after night, if the world would be better off if I found a way to leap from the top of that very same chapel.

Eventually, I did find a sense of community through my club soccer team and a rag-tag comedy group I joined. I made a new

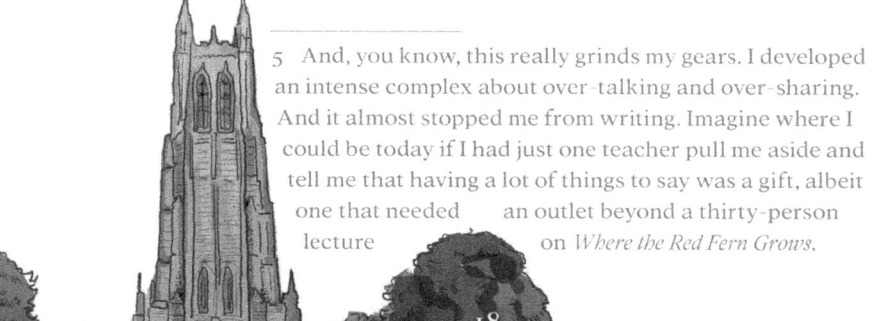

5  And, you know, this really grinds my gears. I developed an intense complex about over-talking and over-sharing. And it almost stopped me from writing. Imagine where I could be today if I had just one teacher pull me aside and tell me that having a lot of things to say was a gift, albeit one that needed an outlet beyond a thirty-person lecture on *Where the Red Fern Grows*.

plan. I wouldn't come out to anyone at Duke. I would hold on to my secret for four years, I would become financially independent shortly thereafter, and I would move to a new town and live my gay life in secret—a lesbian recluse fabled to be living in the hills. I would essentially be the gay Oprah, with a national audience wondering why she can't get a man.

This plan helped me survive the first semester of school. But just barely. I was living a double life, and every so often, I would fall apart. If I was home for a break, I would collapse into my mother, sobbing, an anxious mess.

On New Year's Day, eating breakfast at my parents' kitchen counter, my mom asked me what my resolution was. I told her that I was going to try to do better in school. But I made a silent promise to myself that 2012 was the year I would come out.

Then, by the time I finished my pancakes, I was back to being straight.

During the spring semester, I signed up for an economics course and caught sight of a girl named Paige. She was tall, blond, and was wearing the matching black sweatsuit designated for Duke athletes, which inspired in me a sense of longing that I could no longer pass off as envy; I didn't want to be her, I wanted to be with her. I thought to myself, "If I could be with someone like this, then I guess coming out wouldn't be so bad." It was a grain of hope that I kept in my back pocket. And with hope came a sort of cautious curiosity that made its presence known in the back of my mind.

In the fall, when I returned to school for my sophomore year, I was once again caught in the limbo that had caused me to pour into my mother's arms the year before. My crush on Paige made me feel more urgently that I should come out. But with that proximity came a renewed dread. I slumped into a depression. On bus rides to and from the main campus, I would play Macklemore's "Same Love" on repeat. It wasn't the best choice, but I was desperate for any media that would allow me to understand what I was experiencing.

There was a lot about the song that spoke to me. His commentary on stereotypes felt important, as I had troubled myself thinking that I didn't look like any lesbian that I had ever seen on television. His observation that we use *gay* as an insult called up all the moments in which I had heard jokes about lesbians, which would make me laugh and then cause a sharp pain in my chest. It also brought to mind all the times my sister's friends used *dyke* as the lowest possible form of degradation.

Perhaps most poignant to me was the line he sings about kids who "would rather die than be who they are."

There were a handful of queer narratives out there—I saw Kurt come out on *Glee*, I saw Michael Scott kiss Oscar on *The Office*—but I had never seen someone grappling with their own identity. I had never seen in anyone else the paralysis I was feeling. I clung with a white-knuckled grip to the hope that I could meet one single boy whom I might want to kiss. I knew—I *knew*—I was gay. But I didn't *want* that.

Did I get no say?

About halfway through the semester, a senior on the club soccer team, Robin, noticed my apparent mood shift. Robin reminds me a bit of Dory from *Finding Nemo*. Besides her big blue eyes that are always wide with excitement, she is squirrelly and crazy and will decide to cross an entire ocean in a heartbeat. She is also kind and caring in a way that often gets overlooked.

The team called her "Mother Blobbin." An unconventional mother, sure, known for picking up freshmen late on a weeknight and forcing them to do a beer bong. She chauffeured teammates around on their twenty-first birthdays so that she could watch over them while they, most certainly, drank so much they hurled their guts out; then she picked up the birthday girl the morning after, with Gatorade, coffee, maybe donuts, definitely a trash can. Being with Robin is like feeling the thrill of imminent danger but also feeling safe and watched over. Put simply, there's no one like her.

Robin and I, along with some other girl named Leah, were goalies and spent a fair amount of time together. One night, not so long into my sophomore slump, she asked if she could drive me home. I knew that a conversation about my mental health was coming. The toll my double life was taking on me was growing apparent. I wanted Robin to ask after me and I was grateful to know that someone cared. But I didn't know how I would respond without giving myself away. She followed me into my apartment, and, from my kitchen table, she told me that she herself had experience managing depression. She suggested I utilize Duke's Counseling and Psychological Services (CAPS).

At the time, I thought to myself, "I don't have depression, I just don't want to be alive because I'm gay and don't know how to be gay." Of course, I didn't say that. But I did want to tell her something, because I really did need help.

I was a master of long-game strategy. I told Robin, "I can't go see someone because then I'll have to deal with ... *this*."

In one seemingly elongated second, I watched Robin react to my gameplay. And I swear, in an instant, I saw her face go from brow-furrowing confusion to eye-widening clarity. With her eyebrows still reaching for her hairline, she stared at me, knowing full well that I was gay.

This was the defining moment of my coming out—the only one that could clearly separate the before and after. And I had said almost nothing. There had been no letter, no movie.

We talked about continuing this conversation after our Halloween soccer tournament, and she left my apartment. Later that night, I texted Robin: "Thanks. I'm not ready to talk about what's going on just yet, but when I am, I think I would like to talk to you about it." That was my verbal commitment to myself that I was now running toward my issue, instead of away from it.

This began a time in our lives that Robin and I like to call, "Talking about talking about it." Every night, when I had finished meetings for the sketch comedy group I led, Robin would pick me up in her Subaru Forester—the safest place, I think, for a closeted lesbian. And, despite the fact that Robin was not actually gay, it was a stick shift, which just added to my feelings of comfort.

## Annie Krabbenschmidt

We would drive the winding back roads of Durham, North Carolina—pitch dark except for the light Robin's headlights cast on passing pine forests. We would stop by a restaurant called Cookout, where, for five dollars or less, you could buy a "Cookout Tray": a main and two sides. Options for mains were things like chicken tenders, quarter-pounders, and hot dogs. Options for sides were also things like chicken tenders, quarter-pounders, and hot dogs.[6]

Some nights, we would do more homework. We frequented an abandoned conference room in the Public Policy building; the tables were narrow rectangles arranged end to end to make a great, empty square. From around nine at night to at least midnight, Robin would do her engineering homework while I tried to focus on German vocabulary.

More often, I would flop myself onto the table with my arms splayed over the edge, presenting the visual image of my own crucifixion. Far from the silent martyrdom of worthier prophets, I would frequently let out a loud groan or call to Robin as though I was on my deathbed, uttering my last words. Perhaps a nearing oblivion would have given me the sense of freedom I needed to say what we both knew was weighing on me.

I did end up going to CAPS, and Robin sat next to me when I made the appointment. I put it in my planner in letters that spelled out a doomsday. Opening up about my feelings didn't inherently intimidate me—I had talked to my high school's counselor about rapid weight loss and had previously talked to someone at CAPS about how homesick I was during my first

---

6   Or corn dogs, or quesadillas, or hushpuppies, or a fried chicken wrap. The list simply does not end.

semester—but the waiting room overlooking Duke's student center was a very brutal who's who of high achieving pressure cookers like myself. And what if they all knew I was there with a case of lesbianism?

But on the day of my appointment, I sat in a private corner staring at my intake form, which had one or two questions about sexuality. Like my first conversation with Robin, answering an innocuous survey became a game of strategy. To write that I identified as straight would mean that I would have to bring up my sexuality on my own. To write that I identified as gay was out of the question. My final decision was to leave that question blank and make my counselor figure out what that glaring omission could possibly mean.

I had a bald psychiatry student named Luke, and it didn't take him long to land on my presenting issue, bespectacled as he was. He was patient with me but didn't let our initial session end without asking about the cavernous space on my intake form that echoed the obvious back on itself. Tears started to well in my eyes as I apologized for my lack of composure. The most I did by way of confession was to tell him that I was scared to talk about it—that once I talked to him—actually said the words aloud, my secret would become my truth. He suggested I come back once a week.

After my first appointment, Robin asked me if I had talked about "the thing."

I told her that I had and nothing more. The words continued to elude me, but I wasn't shying away from her knowing about "the thing." Perhaps most important was the clear evidence that Robin wasn't abandoning me for being gay. In fact, the more committed we were to my coming out, the more she seemed to stand by my side.

And so did Luke—though, in his case, that was his job. I got slightly more comfortable every time I talked about myself. I was explaining to Luke that I didn't know that I would be sure about my sexuality until I was with someone, but to try and be with someone would require me to announce my sexuality somehow.

"I feel like I'm in purgatory," I said, as casually as my mother would if she were describing an inconvenient layover in Dallas.

Eyes widened and concerned, Luke asked, "Do you really feel that way?"

"No, not really," I said, pitying this man for his poor sense of humor, without realizing that my shame was so intense that he was more right to be concerned than I was to be flippant. My fear of being gay was so great that a logical explanation *would* be that I was a hell-fearing Christian.

Still, it would be a mistake to call this a pure limbo. I wasn't really confused. I was terrified. I had done flight for my entire life, I had done freeze for about a year, and now I was fighting. I was making movement forward, graceless though it was.

As Luke and I worked through the maximum number of therapy sessions that Duke allowed (seven), Robin continued to pick me up, without fail. Our talking about talking about it became a little more detailed, a little more like talking about it. Sometimes we communicated so casually about it that I almost tricked myself into believing that I had already come out; on some nights, when Robin would pick me up from the library to begin our wanderings, I imagined that I would open her car door and just say, "That's it, I'm gay!" Approaching the passenger side, however, always had a way of deflating me.

After a month or more, the drawing out of the process approached the ridiculous. In a way, I had trapped myself into moving forward. I continued to give Robin pieces, concretizing a reality that could only be destroyed by lying outright. And frankly, I've never been a good liar.

By the middle of November, we were staying up until three or four in the morning. For weeks, Robin had devoted her time to me, making me chicken parmesan dinners and keeping me company in between our drives. Keeping her up until daybreak felt like the very last straw—I owed her action. So, on the morning of November 17, as the sun was beginning to come up, painting the sky in a dull pink—the sunrise was much less cinematic than I had hoped it would be—I told her I was ready.

Of course, as I sat trying to form words, I realized they wouldn't come out of my mouth. I found a takeout napkin in Robin's cup holder. As I sat poised to write, the words still wouldn't come. I realized I would need a little privacy. I climbed in the backseat of the car. I was ready. Except one last touch, which was that I needed to have a very specific Neil Diamond song[7] playing while I wrote—perhaps my coming out would be dramatic after all.

*Just in case you're looking to enhance your reading experience*

---

7   A song that I knew from a scene in *Zoolander*, in which a despondent Derek gives up his career as a male model and tries to reconnect with his coal-mining father and brothers.

So, finally, I wrote my letter.

"Okay well this is really weird," I began. "I'm 90% sure I'm gay." I wrote the word so small that I hoped Robin might miss that tiny detail. And on I went, as Neil sang about a road with no known destination.

When Robin finished reading, she looked into the backseat to find me with steady tears coming down my face.

"You did it," Robin said. "I'm proud of you."

When Neil Diamond finished, I played Robin my song—"Same Love." It's an odd thing, to ask someone to contemplate your emotional artifacts; to understand that for months, a five-minute song tethered you to breathing. I tried to point out each line's significance to her. What a stereotype meant to me, what the word *dyke* meant to me, that I was so unhappy I could die.

Robin could never fully understand most of these things. But considering that no one had ever come out to her before, she came awfully close.

· X · X · X ·

I wish that I could say that coming out freed me. I was finally able to share my private gay-related humor with Robin, which felt good, but laughter is not always the same as relief. I still felt depressed. Within a few days, I was back on her couch, feeling that the world was crushing my chest, no better off than I had been the previous year.

And I sobbed to her. I mean, really sobbed. I heaved air in and wailed it out. It was the first time I really, *really* cried about my terror. The kind of crying that controls you, rather than the other way around.

"I don't want to do this," I said to her. "I wish I had never told you." I was bound to a reality in which at least one person knew that I was attracted to women, and that is what really made me "gay." Robin calmly told me that I didn't have to tell anyone else if that's what I wanted, but we both knew it wasn't.

She had me write a list. All the reasons I had wanted, and still wanted, to come out. I started:

1. Change things for people I know
2. I want to be a role model
3. I can provide an alternative to stereotypes

At the bottom of the list—the seventh or eighth item—was the possibility that coming out might make me happier. Robin shook her head at me. "This list is all backwards," she said. I had no idea what she meant. I didn't know what happiness had to do with any of that. Being out and gay felt more like a chore than anything else.

The next night, Robin arrived with her signature look of "I'm going to make you do something epic." With her Dory eyes, she told me that she had an idea of how to make me feel better.

She had bought a number of glass items from the dollar store and took me to a deserted roof somewhere in the Engineering quad. We dropped wine glasses and sealed pickle jars from the roof just to watch them shatter. I hurled small vases against a brick wall. We laughed at ourselves.

Robin beamed. "You feel better, right?!"

Sadly, I didn't. I was still gay, and the life that lay ahead of me still terrified me. And someone was going to have to pick up those glass pieces and those pickles.

I spent the next semester, Robin's last at Duke, doing a film program in California—convenient for someone who wants to get away fast. Before I left, Robin threw me a surprise going-away party. There were all the teammates who had become my family—who, Robin assured me, would still love me when the time came to come out to them, whenever it was that I wanted to do that.

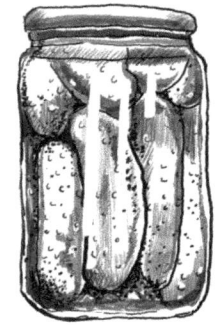

I only came out to two more people that fall. Because we were going to be roommates on the main quad when I got back from LA, I wanted to tell Leah ahead of time, to give her an opportunity to change her mind—which, of course, I considered a likely possibility. But I had yet to say the words *I'm gay* out loud.

Robin recommended that I practice coming out to her roommate, "because she went to an all-girls school, so she'll know what to do." We called an apartment meeting, and I sat across from sweet Ruthie for about ten minutes, hemming and hawing before finally telling her.

"Okay ..." she said, waiting for something more.

"Well, you went to an all-girls school ..." I trailed off before turning on Robin. *"Ruthie will know what to do?"* I parroted. "Are you kidding me?!"

Robin threw her hands up. "Do you think I have any idea of how to do this?" We sat laughing (my laughter dripping with a very specific kind of mortification) while Ruthie wondered if she could get back to her homework.

My meeting with Leah didn't go much better. We had soup before class one day, and as my cup sat untouched and cold, I struggled to let the words come up my throat and out of my mouth.

Whether she was nervous or not, she said she wanted to live with me anyway. Sure, we spent the first few months respectfully changing in the privacy of our dorm room closet—because, as was the case with Robin, neither of us had a clue as to how to handle my sexuality—but Leah became my very best friend, and ultimately, my relationship with her has been one of the most important and authentic of my life; perhaps specifically because she loved me when I was her teammate, when I was a nervous closeted lesbian, when I was in the annoying stages of my first relationship, when I was in the annoying stages of my first break up, and, finally, when I started to heal from all of these events.

Robin sent me off to California with a new playlist—all the songs I would need to remember that I was going to make it: Wilson Phillips's "Hold On," The Proclaimers' "I'm on My Way," and John Parr's "St. Elmo's Fire (Man in Motion)." All carried the very subtle message of "keep going, you got this, because you can do anything when there's a key change involved." Someone who *knew* I was gay said that!

I didn't do it on purpose, but I had forced Robin to watch at excruciating proximity what it meant for me to come to terms with my sexuality. She never winced, and she never looked away.

She looked right at me. And she kept looking as I chased one girl, then the next—as I chased one dream then the next—not like I was a freakshow, but like I was a kid whose presence on this earth wasn't such a bad thing.

# Coming Out in Love

I N *LIVING A Feminist Life,* the scholar Sara Ahmed uses the metaphor of a river to represent our culture—the great, flowing force of which carries us all along in some vague uniformity. But not all of us belong in the waters we tread. For example, I would not make the same choice as my parents to dress your family up in a matching plaid pattern for the holiday card, and yet, somewhere in the bottom of a desk drawer, there is a picture of me as a child, wearing tears and tartan.

The writer Alice Gregory documented her time at Switzerland's last finishing school for *The New Yorker*, and in her subtle mockery I saw a very realistic articulation of my childhood. For the attendees of Institut Villa Pierrefeu (IVP), the social and professional world was one to *master*. I recognized in her description of the students' determination to learn all twenty-five levels of English peerage the same discipline it took me to keep track of divorces, facelifts, and civil forfeitures. From the age of two, I attended Yacht Club functions and dinner parties. We took elaborate vacations to European cities, where we would get dressed up and dine in the world's best restaurants, my innocence spoiled too early when my mom gave the American translation for escargot one bite too late.

During the week, I attended a private K-8 school with an immaculate exterior, painted white and lined with navy. The school was so pristine that even its attendees appeared to be part of the design scheme as we walked in two evenly spaced parallel lines from one class to the next, our white collared shirts tucked in, our hands behind our backs, and our socks never *ever* falling below our ankles.

It is a world of social decorum; the rules are subtle but strict and the consequences are enormous. In summary, I think that in my world, sexuality—especially the gay kind—was something that we all just pretended didn't exist.

Now, I had previously *experienced* queerness. I just didn't realize it at the time. But in retrospect, it seems so obvious that I had been in love with Cristine McGray from the first day of kindergarten to the last day of eighth grade. She had straight blond hair and, lest you think me superficial, glasses.

At naptime, every nap time, I positioned my blanket and pillow right under her cubby so that I could memorize the very precise way she spelled her name. In fact, I remember little else of kindergarten except for the teacher-written, perfectly rounded, black Sharpie lettering on the tag next to her plastic pencil case.

I never would have acknowledged that I was attracted to Cristine,[8] but at the same time, I didn't know that I was experiencing

---

8   I remember very little of eighth grade besides Sandra Allen calling me a lesbian under her breath, which, being the height of insult, prompted me to spray my Treetop apple juice carton in her face. You think she struck a nerve?

desire—or what, even, desire was. Just like all my friends, I loved *The Notebook*. And I went weak when Ryan Gosling spits through the rain that "it wasn't over, it still isn't," just like all my friends. But did all my friends also notice that for about three quarters of a second during that scene, you can catch a glimpse of what I believed was Rachel McAdams's right nipple? I didn't ask.

And was it curiosity that made me watch it again and again, or was it attraction? I rewound that scene so often my DVD might as well have had "it's your sexuality, stupid" etched into its grooves.

Almost a decade later, when I saw Paige carefully selecting a seat in our Introduction to Political Economy class, my world stopped. Well, my world—the river I trudged along in—didn't stop, but I had the sudden urge to stand and resist the flow of normalcy.

She was tall, almost awkwardly so, with perfectly straight blond hair, which she wore in an athletic-looking braid, made all the more legitimate by her actual Duke Lacrosse warmups. Her eyes were a deep brown, her skin was perfect, and her cheeks were always a little flushed. She did not have glasses, and she was a little plain in the sense that she lacked any distinguishing features except her nose, which was almost imperceptibly hooked. She was the most beautiful person I had ever seen. One[9] could even argue[10] that she was out of my league. She somehow reminded me of all the girls I had ever loved and all the girls I had ever wanted to be, all at the same time.

---

9    My sister.

10   Still, to this day.

So, I did what any lovesick nineteen-year-old would do after they've made a pledge to themselves to confront their feelings for women: I spent the next eighteen months of my life blurring the line between stalking and courtship in an effort to get closer to her.

And I'm not saying that I have a proven strategy, okay, but I am saying that nine years after learning to spell her name, I had the chance to stroke Cristine McGray's cheek when I played her uncle in the eighth-grade production of *Guys and Dolls*. I am always prepared for the long game.

And, rather fortuitously, so was Paige.

In fact, not so long into our friendship she confessed that she remembered meeting me in our dorm building in the first weeks of school. She had found my DukeCard next to the common room printer, and when she handed it back to me, had said, "Awesome last name!" Ironically enough, I was too distracted by the realization that I was a lesbian to remember our very first encounter, but when I heard this story the following spring, I thought that it had been fate herself leading me into that classroom.

Now, if you felt that I was overthinking my coming out strategy, you might want to skip ahead. Or, actually, you might want to return this book.

My friendship with Paige started off normal enough. Besides the fact that we lived in the same dorm, on a bus ride back to the first-year campus, we discovered that we loved all the same NBC comedies.

Such casual and commonplace conversation. It would be a shame if someone were to ... go overboard with that kind of information.

It was me. I went overboard.

I created a ringtone from the *30 Rock* theme song in the hope that someone might call me while I was in her presence. Since no one actually uses the phone to make calls, my plan snagged. I recovered by setting a timer to go off in the middle of class. That definitely got her—and seventy-four other people's—attention.

I wondered, when was a good time to friend her on Facebook? A month seemed like a good amount of time, but if that was the right time to wait before sending an innocent friend request, then why hadn't *she* sent one herself?

After talking myself up, and deciding that if she wasn't gay then she wouldn't think anything of one tiny friend request, I wandered over to her profile.

There it was.

Her banner photo on Facebook was for a political campaign denouncing North Carolina's recent ban on same-sex marriage. I decided that Paige was gay because no one I had ever known in high school had so openly expressed support of queer people.

When she accepted my friend request, I posted on her Facebook wall, asking if she wanted to study for our midterm together. She gave me an enthusiastic yes. Months later, I would come to find out that she hated studying with other people, but that night found the two of us reciting, over and over again, the lyrics to a YouTube rap battle video called "Fear the Boom and Bust: Keynes vs. Hayek on economic theory."

When, in the middle of the study session, she mentioned that Taco Bell had a new Dorito-flavored taco shell, I spent an hour making a Zipcar account so that at 11:00 p.m., the two of us could go on a quest to find the most mediocre tacos in all the land.

As it turns out, Paige hated group studying *and* Taco Bell, but those are the kind of romantic lies you can talk about at a party when you tell the story of how you and your partner met. In contrast, my ringtone maneuver was something so contrived, I had to write a whole book to explain what it was about Paige Henderson that made me do it. This was my first attempt at real flirting.

Though we exchanged numbers at some point in the spring, our interactions remained sparse and chaste for the rest of the semester. But when I passed her in the hallways as I packed up my belongings at the end of freshman year, I felt like she was the only person I would miss that summer.

One day in the middle of July, I thought about kissing her.

· X · X · X ·

The following fall was the semester I spent coming out to Robin. This was no coincidence. When I told Luke, the psychiatry student, about Paige, he proposed that I had created this crush out of nothing. Many people, he explained, conjure crushes on people of their same gender when they are exploring their sexualities.

What he didn't understand was that my coming out story began and ended with her. For all intents and purposes my sexuality was, "sitting on separate couches with Paige."

We did that a lot back then. Praise Tina Fey, the final season of *30 Rock* was airing on NBC that fall. We were perhaps the only two college students watching live television, but every Thursday, I would walk to her dorm building and text her to let me in

while I tried to find a casual way to lean against the handrailing.

Praise another deity that Leah also happened to be a barista for the cafe near Paige's dorm. On Wednesdays, I would do work there while my stone-faced friend attempted to deliver dry wit and cappuccinos to the students of West Campus. Six times out of ten, Paige would come strolling in at some point during the evening to conveniently find me with my German textbook open to a page of little consequence because, really, when was I going to need directions to the Bahnhof?

At 5'10" she had a gait that allowed her to walk slowly while covering distance, and it was almost casual. Most times, she never even slowed her pace while we talked as she sauntered to the elevator bank. It was the best minute and a half of my day.

Then I would head back to my apartment, which was a full thirty-minute journey away and included a short bus ride. Leah was, somehow, none the wiser and was genuinely shocked when I came out to her.

In her defense, I always had a good excuse for walking into that coffee shop.

"What am I doing here?" I might say while picking up the nearest item for sale. "I'm just grabbing an Almond Joy. A candy that everyone loves."

Toward the end of the semester, as athletes loosened their rules, I started seeing Paige out. I say "seeing out" as if the entire school didn't know that varsity athletes always spent Wednesday nights at Shooters Saloon, the only eighteen and over bar in town.

Emboldened by coming out to Robin, I would go there to find her. To aid in my efforts, Robin would call every member of the team to try and convince them to go out with us. Sometimes we only got freshmen, but if I got to see Paige for a single second, I was happy.

Sometimes we even hugged because we were both so, like, totally wasted.

Come spring, I left Duke to spend a semester at film school in Los Angeles. Was it a convenient way to avoid dealing with my sexuality and my crush on Paige? Yes. Is that why I went out of my way to enroll in an entirely new program three thousand miles away? I mean, it's really hard to say.

But sure, it's possible.

It's bittersweet to think of that time. I toured the studios of shows I loved, met with Duke alums in the *industry*, read scripts—I basically had the world at my feet. But all I could think about was getting back to my dorm room for my biweekly texting date with Paige.

And I do mean that, without fail, we talked twice a week: Tuesdays and Fridays.

We never had an appointment. But what started subtly ("Are you in LA yet?" "Yes! Do you think Delta Gamma[11] will survive

---

11  Yes. It's true. I was briefly a Delta Gamma.

without me?") became an unspoken agreement. We took turns initiating with some useless intro text. We never discussed feelings (for each other or otherwise) and we texted for hours. Eventually, one of us would have to go to sleep. Usually me, at 2:00 a.m. Which was 5:00 a.m. for Paige.

But it was that commitment—the fact that she showed up every week, that she kept moving forward with me—that felt like love. Either of us could have easily fallen off the face of the earth, for fear or lack of interest, and there would be almost no consequence (except for a most excruciating devastation). We owed each other nothing.

I don't recommend beginning a relationship this way. Bantering via text for twelve hours straight is fine for a couple weeks, but not so much for eight months. And yet, that was what we most needed.

As the fall semester approached, I knew that the time for action was near. In Ahmed's river, we were starting to move against the flow. You don't run through a rushing river, you slog. Slowly, coordinated. There was no need to talk about the pressure of the river pushing against us—we felt it.

Oh, we felt it.

Sexual tension by any other name would be just as taut, even if from across the country.

As fate, that interfering cupid, would have it, when I got back to school for my junior year, my new dorm room window literally faced hers.

There was a feeling in the air, and "anticipation" wouldn't even begin to encapsulate it. Our courtship was no longer sustainable, even if only because the emotional build would have nowhere else to go now that it had ballooned against all the walls we had put up to stay safe.

And yet.

When I was with her, it was easy to forget the danger of being in love with her.

"Scootin'" is what Leah called it.

I went to Paige's room every night for about a month. If I saw that her light was on, I texted her asking if she wanted to hang out, and every time, she responded that she did. The first time, we sat on opposite sides of her king bed, which was really two dorm twins pushed together.

After nearly a year and a half, it came down to this: two bodies steadily moving closer together, one inch a night.

When I had dated Aiden, my Model UN hunk, it took all my strength to get near enough to his body to actually touch—which is probably why he ended up hitting my turned cheek instead of my mouth during our first kiss. With Paige, I couldn't help it; I wanted be nearer to her than I had been the night before. That, it dawned on me, is why they call it attraction.

The first time our hands touched, it was when mine rested in hers to show her a video on my phone, the latest Apple product clearly too heavy for one little hand to lift it alone.

Then our socked feet were nestled together.

Then, eventually, our bodies found each other.

And then, finally, we held hands—an act that is modeled innocently in straight friendships, when two women are very drunk and in between frat party locations, but not late at night, in the awkward tension of full sobriety, between two certified non-touchers.

We never spoke about what was happening or dared to identify our feelings. We held hands for a full week without saying a word, but every night we clung more forcefully to each other. And when I felt scared, I simply held her tighter.

Finally, *finally*, she broke the silence, telling me that she "liked me." Breathing a huge sigh of relief, I felt deeply indebted to her for being the braver of us. So, I kissed her, both of our lips stiffly pursed and dry. And from then on out, almost everything was easy, and when it wasn't, it was manageable because we had each other.

We had trudged upstream together. We took slow, calculated steps toward real authentic love. Certainly, it must have occurred to her, as it did to me, multiple times a day, that this journey was absurd.

But if she had asked me on a date when we had met, eighteen months prior, I'm sure I would have panicked. I'm also sure she felt the same way. Instead, we challenged each other to move forward with intentional, smooth steps. Maybe not "smooth," per se—during one class meeting shortly after we became friends, I tried, very coolly, to toss some Nerds candy in my mouth and instead spilled the entire box out onto the table we shared—but we moved as carefully and safely as we could toward a life we couldn't have imagined just two years before.

So, I didn't have a jock boyfriend, but I was over the moon to have my jock girlfriend. I went to every single game I could, alongside the two or three other Duke students interested in women's sports—unless, of course, there was some sort of torrential downpour, in which case I stood alone in my bright red rain shell.

And I loved being her girlfriend. I loved introducing her as my girlfriend. I loved getting the occasional (and coveted) invite to attend team events as her plus one. Everything—all the fear, all the feelings that I was some kind of freak—they quieted.

Both of us marveled at the fact that we didn't feel particularly gay. And of course, what does the word *gay* signify when it's shared in the privacy of two people madly in love? Every gratuitous declaration of feelings felt as though it had sprung from deep inside my heart—like I had never rolled my eyes when a film character says, "You take my breath away."

Kissing, which had always left me underwhelmed and slobbery, really felt like the connecting of two souls. I don't have much to say except that being with Paige changed me, as if every ion in my body had flipped its charge, because I saw the world now as its inverse.

If there is a high concentration of artists in the queer community, maybe it's because some of us went from staying in

the closet, hoping that normative success symbols would fulfill us, to seeing that all their promises would fail to make us whole. Those of us who came out of the closet begrudgingly decided that love was our most precious resource.

And even though Paige and I would eventually have a very messy break up, I was head-over-heels in love with her, period. I just want to sit for a moment in how wonderful it is to know love, to feel love within you. Because the knowledge of that feeling never goes away.

I think of her often and fondly, and I think about the love I had for her, and I sometimes wonder if I would still take a bullet for her, and honestly, I think I would. As easily as I can recall my own name, I remember every detail of our coming together, from sentence to sensation. I remember leaving her dorm room in my ratty sweats, hopping two steps at a time down the stairwell. I remember being closer to a human body than I had ever been before. I remember reading love letters and thinking, "Is this really for me?"

You can't unknow that feeling. If there was hurt, it is overwhelmed by my memory of joy. She was one of a kind. Objectively brilliant, talented in so many ways, curious, thoughtful, and loving.

It was the perfect love story. Still is.

# Coming Out of Love

*-or- A Lacanian model for reverse castration toward lesbian jouissance*

### ANNIE KRABBENSCHMIDT
*Director of Arts and Craft, Bread People Productions*

### Abstract:

*It was the perfect love story. Still is. But stories don't just appear out of thin air. We craft them. And the person (me) who crafted the "perfect" love story between two closeted lesbians was also a real Twilight fan and fell prey to her own obsession with the Swan/Cullen human/vampire dilemma. In this essay, I will critique Meyer's theory of obsessive love between human and vampire as "unrealistic" and "deeply problematic," and argue that we should stop romanticizing it, particularly in the mind of a young, repressed lesbian. As a next best alternative, Bella should have chosen Jacob Black, the werewolf-cum-boy, who would have allowed her to keep her life (socio-familially and literally) intact.*

**Keywords:** *lesbian; enmeshment; self-loathing; ego death.*

## Introduction

*Twilight* is something I think about a lot, but until now, I have not made that plain in a public setting. That's because there's something silly that happens on college campuses, especially places like Duke, where we're all trying to prove to one another that we are excellent. Of course, on paper, we all kind of look the same. Same grades, same leadership roles, same AP scores. If anything, the fact that I actually failed the AP US History Exam might be something that helped me stand out.

When everyone's admissions file looks so similar, there is simply no choice but to out-intellectualize your peers so you can give off the impression that you are *genuinely* smart and did not fail any Advanced Placement exams. This is how I ended up becoming a major in the critical theory department.

The curriculum was your standard Lacan, Butler, Adorno, Engels, and Marx, with their arguments over subject castration and sublime phenomenology (you know, the useful stuff); because, I figured, if I couldn't master the philosophical musings of these old German men, then I might not be very intelligent at all.

The truth, disappointing as it was to discover, was that I could gain nothing—no knowledge, no wisdom, no guidance—from my studies. I do not know what *phenomenology* means, let alone how to identify it as sublime. But, for funsies, I have attached Lacan's graph of desire, presented here as *Figure 1*. Instead, most of my insights on the subject of codependency will be coming directly from my understanding of *Twilight*, which—unlike my knowledge of Lacan—is quite expansive.

## Castration—or—Edward Singles Out the New Girl

I remember devouring the *Twilight* series. Late at night, I would read and reread passages that were particularly tantalizing. Being twelve, I didn't realize that what I was experiencing would be considered sexual excitement. But getting off to that book must have really messed me up because I was adamantly Team Edward and it *showed*.

I watched the movie recently and every word that comes out of that vampire's mouth is something that should warrant a restraining order. But at the time, I was enthralled by the story of love between a vampire and the woman he has chosen as his one true mate: Bella Swan, a clumsy, misunderstood wallflower, who decides, at seventeen, that she's going to marry Edward and also join the vampire coven.

Edward's behavior is like that of an overly possessive partner committing acts of major emotional manipulation. See *Figure 2*. And while he "can't forgive himself" for separating Bella from her human life (including the unsung hero of the series, her father, Charlie), he does very little to stop that from happening.

And we thought that was *romantic*.

There are *millions* of Twilight fans out there that would choose Edward.

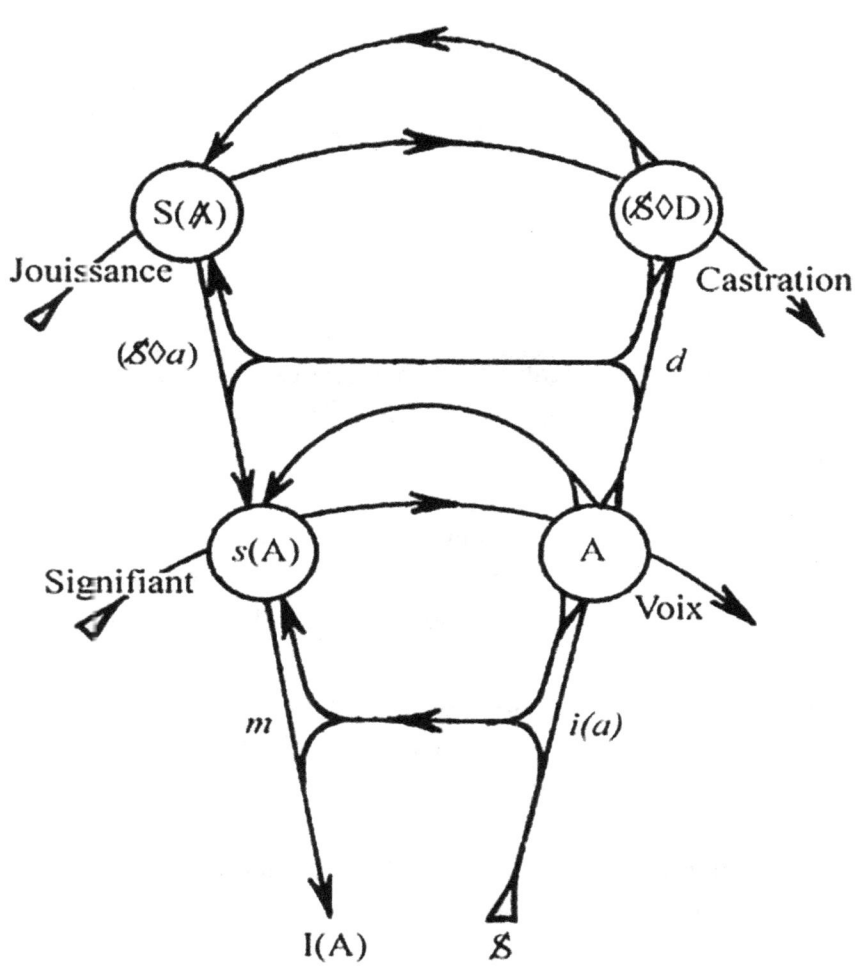

*fig. 1: Lacan's Graph of Desire*

Annie Krabbenschmidt

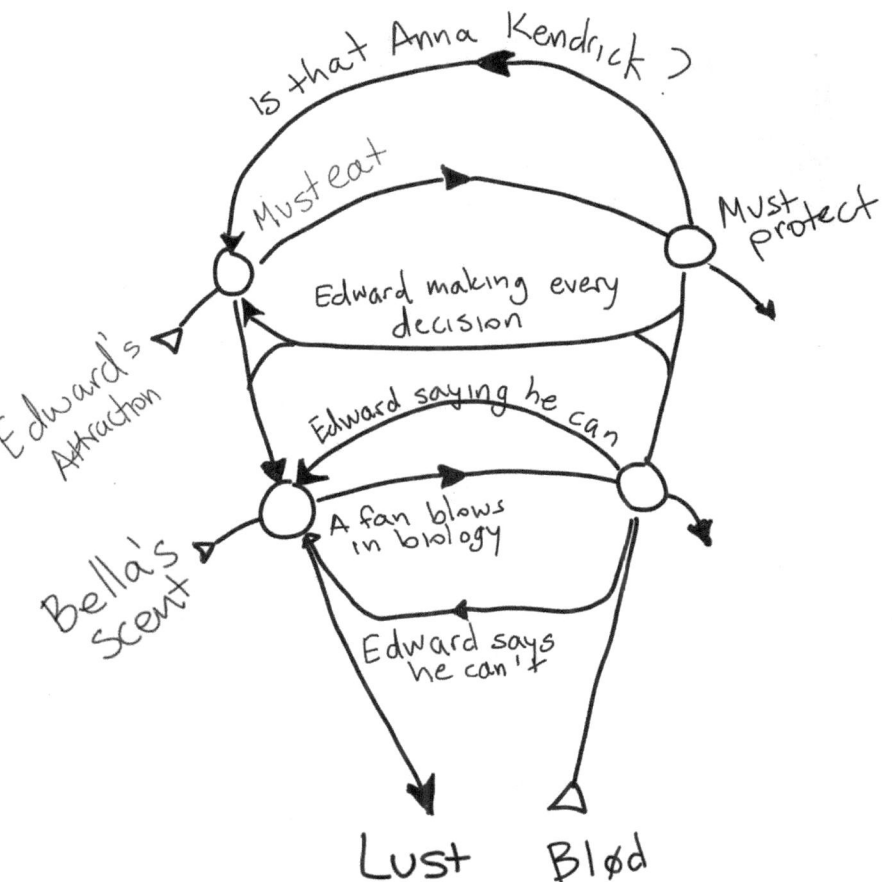

*fig. 2: Edward's Graph of Blødlust*

See Image 1.

Generally, the media endorses this kind of romance. We love the idea of a clandestine soulmate or a spontaneous cross-country move. When I first read that Edward had been watching Bella sleep for weeks before they finally got together, I remember hoping that I was worthy of that kind of desire. I, like Bella, would have happily abandoned friends, family, and country in order to be with "the one." Falling in love and transitioning into lifelessness is a lot like what happened to me (and probably many others) in my first relationship.

*Image 1: People, not me, but people obsessing over Edward Cullen*

The heteronormative social condition (HSC affects millions of families every year; seek help if you think you may be struggling) presents very specific challenges for LGBTQ young folks, which their straight families cannot prepare them for. Where a normative straight couple might struggle to communicate, a queer one might never *stop* processing how one person felt when the other said, "I think I need some alone time tonight."

Paige and I were each experiencing our first queer relationships, which started while both of us were in the closet. Our interactions were inherently anxiety-fueled. While that's generally true for most young courtships—butterflies, spilling down your front, stumbling over words—in ours, there was a layering of many fears. Either one of us could discover that the other 1) was not actually interested, 2) was not actually queer, 3) actually hated lesbians, or 4) might start a campus wide outing campaign. *And*, even though we did eventually end up liking each other, we didn't know how the people in our lives were going to react. Which we knew was probably going to be *fine*, but we had both had locker room experiences wherein some teammate talked about how unlucky it would be to have a lesbian amongst the group.

As we were society's unlawful sexual deviants, our relationship had an inherent isolation to it, not unlike the secrecy of a vampire-human courtship. Even as recently as 2012, there weren't a lot of queer characters or narratives that could offer guidance about what makes for a healthy relationship between two women. For example, we didn't know how discreet a gay couple was supposed to be. We were really *weird* in public settings: we avoided physical contact, we spoke in hushed tones, we didn't dare do a karaoke duet to *Rent*'s "Take Me or Leave Me."

And if it wasn't made clear up to this point, I will state plainly that I am very much someone who wants to sing musical soundtracks on stage.

But I was so happy, so *grateful*, to be loved by somebody, finally, that I barely noticed that I was slowly becoming less of the person I tend to be when I'm at my best.

I often had a choice to make: life or love. As a senior in college, I could either spend the night doing some dorm room introspection or I could choose my love bubble. The love bubble rarely lost. This pattern repeated itself in other aspects of my life. If I was feeling frustrated at club soccer practices or sketch comedy meetings, I just skipped them and sought the good feels of affection instead. Whenever life threatened to get real with me—for instance, "What's your passion? What would you do if money wasn't an issue? What color IS your parachute?"—I could just shrug my shoulders and head over to my girlfriend's apartment to feel validated.

It wasn't healthy. Part of me knew it was not, but the other part of me couldn't stop it from happening. Our relationship blossomed but as a living, breathing, developing human, I did not. It was codependency, and I was at the mercy of my desperation.

I used my relationship to defer work on self-actualization and medicated the more overwhelming parts of entering adulthood by focusing on her needs. Instead of worrying about who I was going to be in the future, I took solace in the fact that at least I knew who I was going to be *with*. It sounds dramatic, but I grew increasingly confused about my own personhood. The more confused I got, the more I clung to my relationship—much to my girlfriend's chagrin, as she preferred that I did *not* cling to her (particularly in public). This cycle sustained itself tenuously until its eventual, and unsurprising, combustion. I honestly can't even blame Paige for how quickly she jumped out of that relationship when given the chance. I was down and was trying my best to drag her down with me.

### Lack—or—Edward Abandons Bella after His Brother Tried to Eat Her

The truth was that Paige and I weren't that great together. She was my best friend, my soulmate, the great love of my life, sure. But we were not thriving. Her competitive, driven, high-achieving nature did not always mesh with the whole "once, I accidentally went to class with a bright blue thong attached to me after it had fused to my pant leg in the dryer" thing that I had going on. I am a silly, *silly* goose, and she could not afford to engage in silliness.

She was kind of a big fucking deal at school and I think will be a big fucking deal in her life. I don't think I appreciated how important that was for her. I didn't understand that her relationship with her coaches was a professional one—that they were literally funding her education in exchange for performance. And, as a result, I tended not to respect that that was the life she wanted for herself. Whatever field she's ended up in, I'm sure it requires a great degree of professionalism. And while I love that for her, I would have hated it for me.

The point is, we were doomed to fail as a couple in the long term.

She had too many athletic or academic engagements to attend my shows or games; I grew bitter. She stayed stoic and focused; I became emotionally eruptive. She desperately needed space and I needed validation, desperately.

*Technically*, I broke up with her, but more realistically, it was my heart and world that were shattered.

Paige and I were on opposite sides of the country. She was finishing another year at school. I was belaying small children up a climbing wall in San Francisco. I was determined to find out if Paige really loved me by asking way too much of her.

I was very lost and very needy. I didn't have a good job, I didn't know what I wanted to do, and I really didn't have many friends. Maybe I thought that if I could see her loving me in that Edwardian way, I might have found at least one reason to like myself. I put a *lot* on her as I tried to survive my first year out of school. I prodded her constantly—even if, especially if, I knew she was busy. You could definitely call it manipulation, but that's exactly what insecurity breeds: an appetite for disappointment, and a determination to experience it.

When it seemed that both of us had had our last straw, we got to fighting over text: big serious texts about priorities, values, commitment. She took days to respond, and I would think about throwing my phone against the wall as I waited for information.

Finally, after days of going back and forth, I gave her an ultimatum: if she couldn't start making me feel like more of a priority in her life, I was walking.

I dangled the axe and she cut the string.

This is the text exchange that ended my two-year relationship:

> *ME: It sounds like we might need different things*
> *HER: :/*

Of course, since we were twenty-two-year-olds, her choice to focus on her life, career, and family was the right one. But that's what I can say with hindsight.

I was catatonic when we broke up. People *say* that break ups are like grieving, and you see people go through self-destructive benders when they experience heartache, but I had always assumed that was blown out of proportion.

But of course, what would you do instead? Find out, while eating alone at In-N-Out, that Adele's new album, *25*, had dropped, but wouldn't be on any streaming platforms? Then decide that this *absolutely* necessitated an immediate call to the closest Best Buy to place a hold on Adele's CD? And then drive twenty miles over the speed limit in order to arrive at the store two minutes before closing to pick up a single copy of *25*? And then subsequently bring that *Compact Disc* to a friend's party and request that they play it?

Look, everyone's journey is different.

I thought that people were being dramatic when they talked about heartbreak. But that's because I had never been in love. I did all the clichés, including making "art" out of the experience (see *Figure 3*). I watched television with dead eyes while in my head, I replayed everything that happened between us. I examined everything I did wrong (because I'm a masochist) and imagined a future where my Paige died instead of breaking my heart (because I'm a sadist). I could not make sense of us not being together. Everything in my gut told me that this was wrong and that we needed to be together.

*fig. 3: Fine Art*

It sounds dramatic to say that I wasn't a person without her, but she was the only woman I had ever been with. I discovered a huge part of my identity as her girlfriend. I had invested almost nothing in the parts of my life that didn't involve Paige. Throughout the fall and winter after we broke up, I would reach out to her—sometimes innocuously, sometimes with my tail between my legs. Talking to her was like a salve. Then our conversations would end, and I didn't know when I was going to hear from her, and I would sink deeper into a depression. A graphic representation, worthy of Lacan, would depict my journey as a series of emotional ups and downs (see *Figure 4*).

The downs were bigger than the ups, which resulted in a slow, dragged-out journey to rock bottom. On the way down were two months of "Happy birthday!!" (from me), "Merry Christmas!!" (from me), and "Happy New Year" (frommm, oh yeah, me).

Everyone did everything they could to try and rescue me. My two best friends planned different trips for me to go on, different parties to go to (none of which would allow me to control the music), different plans to look forward to. But I was hollowed out. I couldn't look past my sadness. Everyone was exhausted by me. I was exhausted by me. My mother was really, *really* exhausted by me.

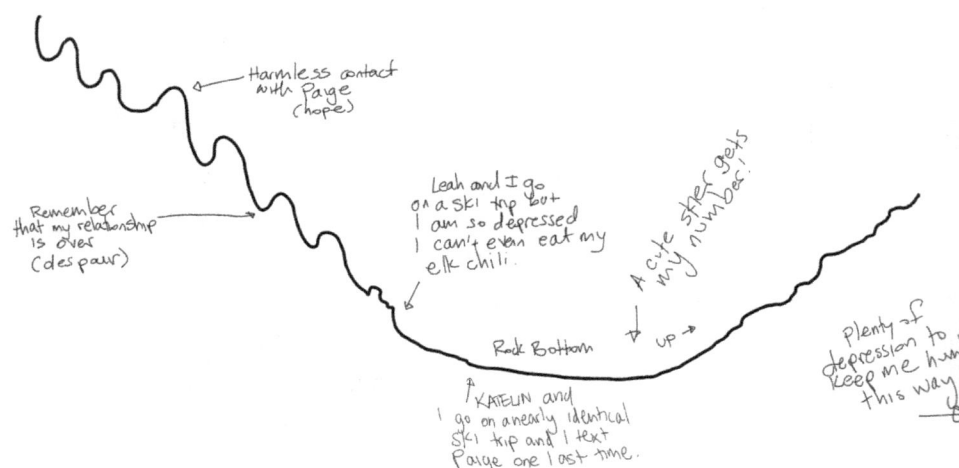

*fig. 4: Annie's Graph of Despair*

I slept in bed with my mom almost every night for more than three months. Amid nonsensical sobbing about how worthless I was, I would confess to her that, yes, I had spoken to Paige recently, and, no, she didn't want to get back together. I told my mom I didn't want to be alive.

I tried to tell her, over and over, that I had nothing—that I *was* nothing. My mom, who had known me long before I became Paige's girlfriend, just did her very best to save me from whatever spiral I was trying to go down on any given night. To her it was unfathomable that I had lost interest in myself. On occasion, she even found my attempts to convince her I was a waste of space so ridiculous that they were funny.

When I told her one night that I wanted to die because I was, in my opinion, "a bum," all she could do was burst into laughter. "A bum!" she repeated, over and over. "I'm a bum. I'm a bum!" We were laughing so hard after that that I could barely get back to my business of hating myself.

But still, I kept clinging to the single hope that Paige would miss being with me. Then one day in January, while I was at a Jackson Hole Moose hockey game with my friend Katelin (one of the many efforts by friends to get me to believe in life after love), I begged Paige in the most shameless way possible to take me back. Via text, I told her that I would be better, I would bother her less, and I would ask for less from her. Essentially, I was willing to compromise my entire person to be with her. When it finally occurred to me that she had meant what she said—that she didn't want to be with me—I let that conversation be our last for a good year.

That night, right on the heels of many dark days, was the worst of my life up to that point. I was in a state of despair, I was panicking, and I was really unsure how I could keep living. Katelin was sleeping peacefully in the neighboring bed while I squirmed with pain and panic. It was so physical, I finally learned why they call it heartache. I didn't sleep; I watched sitcoms, I did breathing exercises, I called my mom twice, and together we grappled with the idea that tomorrow would have to come eventually. I had hit rock bottom.

## Jouissance—or—Girl Seeks Werewolves

We've all heard enough wisdom about rock bottom to know that things started getting better immediately after I hit it. As exhausted as I was, Katelin and I had a very good day together. A cute girl on the ski slopes even asked for my number. She never called, but it was a tiny sliver of hope.

So, I kept snowboarding, I started eating, I laughed a little. I was still sad often. But I was okay. When Katelin and I got back from our trip, we rented a one-bedroom apartment overlooking the most perfect little park in San Francisco. It was one of the best times in my life. Leaving Duke finally allowed me to live without whatever anxious clamp it had once had on my psyche, and I started to see a hint of my better self returning to me. Coincidence or correlation, my life without Duke or Paige was, overall, more joyous than it had been in years. I did stuff that made me feel really elated or excited. I made friends and I did a much better job of showing up for them.

And I dated. I mean, not multiple people (I'm a classic lesbian monogamist, after all), but one very lovely human. As the narrative lords would have it, she was both figuratively and literally warmer than Paige. So you could see why I insisted on bringing *Twilight* into this book in the first place.

I was far from over Paige, so I knew it wouldn't be a long-term relationship, but I cared for Eliza quite a bit. And, most importantly, I was able to bring my needs and my individuality to the forefront of my life. I don't think that's the strategy to maintain a long-term partnership, but I was twenty-two and I had a lot of soul searching to do—which, again, I never could have done while being so head over heels in love.

The years since that heartbreak have been, as most folks' twenties are and should be, the most exciting, devastating, happiest, saddest, loneliest, most unexpected, and most rewarding years of my young life. I owe Paige a great deal of gratitude. This book probably wouldn't exist without her. I'm still bitter that she was right in her conviction that we were *for sure* over, but two people sustain a relationship, not the other way around.

I'm grateful to her for really putting her stake in the ground. I needed her to break my heart fully so that I could start figuring out who I was without her. And in refusing to compromise on herself, she guaranteed that I wouldn't do the same.

In the absence of a partner (though I would have traded anything in the world to have one), I was free to spread my wings a little and find out what new places and people I could see.

Bit of an awkward caveat: the next place I ended up going was not new; I went right back to Durham, North Carolina.

No, I cannot explain why, having realized that I was very miserable in the four years I spent there, that I then went back for a master's at Duke. No, you're not the first person to ask. Like Bella getting back together with Edward, I think I fell back on something familiar—not just the place, but the idea of being a student and, most importantly, getting told what to do with my time.

And all told, I'm pretty pleased with how I did my Duke Redux: as an out, gay, feminist and activist. I wrote op-eds, I gave speeches, I taught classes, and I started writing.

The program wasn't a perfect fit, but my two years back in Durham really brought me so much.[12] I mean, sometimes it was so much agony—the culture wasn't much less perfectionistic than it had been during my undergraduate experience—but at the end, I felt that I had gained quite a bit, triumphed even, in making peace with Duke.

And when I finally left, I felt like I was free.

## Secousse—or—Kristen Stewart Turns Out to Be a Lesbian

But was I free?

Shortly after graduating, I went to New York to take a summer writing class. My sister owned an apartment there and I, once again, found myself graduating from Duke without a consulting gig lined up.

Almost immediately upon arriving in, of all places, the West Village, my sister and our good friend Jacklyn discovered that I had never been to a gay—or lesbian—bar. They looped their arms through mine and marched me straight to the Cubbyhole, a divey lesbian bar a mere quarter mile from my sister's place.

---

12  Leah, that girl I came out to over tomato soup, would have me mention how much fun I had living with her, but I really shouldn't even get started because, obviously, she deserves an entire book all to herself.

While my sister, who had never doubted *her* sexuality, talked to all sorts of women, I sat staring at my cranberry juice, praying no one would approach me.

It had never occurred to me to ask this, since I had been madly in love with and sexually attracted to one, but was it possible that I was scared of lesbians?

The truth is that I may have come out and been out since Paige and I started dating, but I hadn't really come to terms with my sexuality, or myself. I still wanted to be palatable, likable, and easily accepted by the greater Marin County community. I wanted my version of gay to look a lot like my family's version of straight. I wanted my relationship to model exactly like a heterosexual one—HSC striking again.

To return to Sara Ahmed's analogy, the trudging upstream required heft in each step—each planting a declaration that "I'm gay! I'm gay!" which I had always believed a celebration by way of declaration. Truthfully, the motion was more akin to parting through a streaming crowd while saying, to anyone and everyone, "Excuse me. Pardon me." I came out over and over again for the benefit of the stream, as a way to explain my inconvenience. If I could have lifted my head up earlier, I would have seen that on the riverbanks surrounding me, there was a welcome parade. Not the corporate pride parades, where Twitter employees walk trained rainbow parakeets that keep screeching out half-hearted greeting card messages. I'm talking about a hoopla of queers—women shimmying their tatas, the true non-conformists, the artists, and the seedy underbelly of society, parading around. I wish I had noticed them sooner.

I was able to comfortably own the political nature of my identity; it turns out I was still sorting through discomfort around dating and women and dating women. I'm not sure I was ready to actually be rid of the voice inside my head that told me to be ashamed of my sexuality, and ultimately, myself.

Or was it the other way around?

I thought that coming out to my friends and family would be the greatest challenge of my lifetime. Certainly, it felt like the most important part of being gay in North Carolina was stating that I was. And that brave act alone offered me fulfillment—proving to the Duke and Durham community that I was gay and proud was my daily work.

But perhaps there had been a reason, or multiple compounding reasons, why coming out as gay had been so difficult in the first place.

When I walked through the streets of New York, literally teeming with queer people, I suddenly had the realization that I was done coming out.

If Durham was the gawky teenager who has a bold announcement to make at Thanksgiving dinner, the West Village was the cool-butch college senior who buys you your first vibrator. Being gay was not just accepted there, it was unequivocally normal. So, who was I if the main function of my personality was not to simply remind people of my existence?

Excuse me. Pardon me.

I had been living as an apology in every facet of my being. Shame, you might call it.

Unlike guilt, the feeling that you've done something wrong, shame is that feeling that you *are* something wrong.

Coming out of the closet as Annie, or anyone, is more terrifying than introducing someone as your girlfriend. No. I was not scared of lesbians—merely very scared of myself, of being myself, a truly queer human.

It's not "checking the other box;" it's making art out of life and love.

It's scary, sure. I went to a carwash in my hometown wearing my favorite rainbow tie-dye overalls and I got up-downs from lululemon-wearing patrons. A new tattoo could always mean the end of my mother's goodwill toward me. I've been called sir, son, and of course, dyke.

Making the familiar out of foreignness takes a certain amount of steeliness. You're going to face some monsters, both internal and external. But the end result is nothing short of paradise.

In later years, I've watched *Twilight* and insisted that Bella made the wrong choice in Edward. I recognized in their relationship that familiar fragility that I had for so much of my early adult years. I wished that Bella had gotten some more time to get over Edward because I think she might have liked her life.

It took me a while to get there, but I know I've ended up liking mine.

# Concerning Hobbits & Vibrators

IN MY EARLY days as an out homosexual, the one tiny modicum of relief I felt upon accepting that I was—and had all this time been—gay, was that it seemed to explain why I often struggled to fit into girlhood.

Sure, I was a "girl." My grade school's uniform had me wearing a skirt and I used the girls' bathroom; when we lined up in parallel lines to walk from class to class, I walked on the right[13] side, across from whatever boy was so lucky that day. But I was, by the most culturally agreed upon standards, a tomboy. Boyish. I liked building things, climbing things, kicking things.

With freedom, I sometimes chose my own alienation from fellow women. For example, when we would play "Boys vs. Girls" (a game that has no rules, no point, and no victory, except for the successful destruction of Intergender Relations), I played on the boys' team. Through most of my prepubescent years, I geared up for "airsoft war" playdates with Richie, and I had sleepovers in Christopher's treehouse, where he would try to explain a card game called *Killer Bunnies* to me for the umpteenth time.

But this world is never short on reminders that there are ways we are expected to behave. The sleepovers and playdates didn't last long past elementary school and were certainly extinct by the time I went to high school. All those lessons about what being a good girl looked like suddenly became relevant.

It's very possible that this was related to the rising presence, and social importance, of sexual desire.

Now, I knew a *lot* about what makes someone a good girl—a fine lady, even. Just because I preferred to be boyish didn't mean that I hadn't at least *internalized* every behavior my mother and sister modeled for me.

I knew very little, however, about vaginas.

Let me tell you something: having one (a vagina that is), does not entitle you to any understanding about how they work. One would ordinarily rely on an older female figure for mentorship and, frankly, practical information, but recall that I was raised (or supposed to be raised) as a lady. And a real lady doesn't have a "vagina," she has a *secret garden*.

When I was a youth, this is what I knew to be true about S-E-X: A mommy and daddy get married and even though they have probably slept in the same bed before, for some reason the magic of marriage turns the bed into a baby-making machine and eventually a mommy gets pregnant. When I got a little older and saw my Sims have sex a few times—by which I naturally mean that I instructed my Sims to woohoo frequently with their husbands, wives, and unassuming neighbors[14]—I figured out that something about the marital bed involved the particular rubbing of bodies, as indicated by the rumbling of the silver controller of my GameCube Platinum. Then the magic of marriage made a baby possible.

I might have out-Catholic'd some of the best Catholics, and I wasn't even an actual Catholic. But I'll tell you, no one's jaw dropped further than mine when, in my fifth-grade health class, sex was defined as the insertion of a penis *into* a vagina.

"What?!" I yelled quite loudly, hoping that many others would join in a chorus. Alas, this appeared to be a solo act. I looked around in disbelief, hoping to share a moment of bewilderment with my classmates. Nothing. Apparently, everyone had already received this information.

And despite the abject horniness of my Sims avatars, I certainly didn't realize that sex was something for more than making children—that sex could simply be an act of pleasure between two humans.

I'll reiterate that my understanding of the rules of civility condemned open acknowledgement of our bodily functions. Which was fine by me because I was a bedwetter.[15] I slept over at a girl named Paula's house once when I was nine, and when I couldn't find the bathroom in the middle of the night, I just peed where I stood, crying and saying to her, "I'm peeing. I'm peeing." When she gave a very sleepy "okay," I thought I had escaped the worst of my possible embarrassment. Of course, the

---

[14] The mail person, the DJ at the neighborhood party, someone on the same yacht as you, etc., etc.

[15] Feign surprise!

next day, when her mom asked over pancakes if she had heard someone crying in the night, I had to tell the whole table that I had wet her daughter's floor.

My body was just this thing I was stuck lugging around, and it was liable to excretion at any time. When I was eleven, I got my period after school one day and truly believed that I had pooped my pants. Thinking—hoping, even—that was what had happened, I went to school free bleeding the next day. When I got home and checked to see if my underpants were, yup, once again stained, I finally accepted that it was my time. I called my mother in for counsel.

The conversation went something like, "oh my," or "well well," or "ho hum," "wing ding," "beep boop." I don't remember the point at which my mother went from being a human to being a robot, but as I had hardly figured out baby creation, I was, and am, in no position to understand technical advancements in artificial intelligence. She fetched me a pad the size of a rolled-up washcloth and we didn't speak again.

Instead, we watched fourteen hours of *Gilmore Girls*, a show that is famous for its talking but also never mentions vaginas, periods, or pleasure.[16]

And then, on I went with my life (with a very acute anxious attachment to and obsession with Lorelai Gilmore). I navigated the world as a slightly misfitting girl, but for the most part, I got along alright once I figured out how to use tampons. I tended to seek out friends who seemed equally confounded by the *new* rules of Boys vs. Girls that had emerged at puberty. I leaned on sports and shared extracurriculars to find my friends.

---

16  It does, however, make an uncomfortable number of gay jokes. I mean my god, Amy Sherman-Palladino.

# F*r*ed

• X • X • X •

When I was in grad school, a shared interest in trying to make an impact on the world brought some incredible women into my life. Between classes, we discussed far-off regions of the world like Ethiopia, Moldova, and Middle Earth. As we prepared to enter the working world, we plotted a takedown of the patriarchy. These were smart, wonderful people, who actually made me feel proud to *be*, at least to some degree, a woman. For someone who spent many years feeling ostracized from the very notion of womanhood, I was a quick convert to the feminist cause.

I was learning (which involved a great deal of unlearning) that being an ideal woman had nothing to do with the clothes you wear, but rather the magnitude of the misogyny you vowed to take on single-handedly. During the 2016 election, when many criticized Hillary Clinton for being too masculine, robotic, or uncuddly, I saw that she was a more realistic model of woman. That is to say, flawed, ostracized, resilient, and self-assured.

It was in the uneasy calm of that October that my new friends joined me at my house for light fare, half-hearted studying, and  music from the Shire. While merry woodwinds fraternized gaily with an ensemble of stringed instruments, I barely made out the word *anal* as it was spoken aloud by one friend to another. I silently raised my head, careful not to make sudden movements, betrayed entirely by my widening eyes. I wondered if it would be terribly conspicuous of me to reach for earphones, or a handful of pencils, to shove into my ears.

Frozen in space, I glared at the suddenly engrossing utility curves in my economics textbook. Yet now all I could see were nesting phalluses. Despite recently conceding that women were actually quite nuanced beings, I couldn't keep myself from thinking, "How could you?" How had this wholesome study session, accompanied by a *Lord of the Rings* soundtrack, turned into a conversation about sex, which I had grouped together with other uneasy mysteries, like death or dust mites.

When they noticed my tightening lips, they pressed me on why I wouldn't participate in the conversation. I offered them the first thing that came to mind: "Well, I can't contribute much to this conversation because I'm a virgin."[17]

Not even slightly impressed with my purity, my friend, Sarah, who speaks Elvish, guided me through this conversation, which was long overdue. "What about Paige? I assume you two had sex."

"Well, sure," I guessed, "we did stuff."

It was then—sitting with women who knew just as much about the female orgasm as they did about the risks of foreign development missions, while "Concerning Hobbits One Hour" played on YouTube—that I realized that I was not a virgin at all and hadn't been one for quite some time.

While my friends debated whether or not a vibrator was an absolutely necessary purchase, I scanned my mental inventory, wondering how I could have misunderstood such a fundamental detail of my adulthood.

I mean, it goes without saying that no one *explained* to me how two women might go about pleasuring each other. In fifth grade, we had discussed sex mostly as it pertained to procreation.

---

[17] I believe the not-at-all condescending term I was looking for was "Gold Star Lesbian," or, a lesbian who has never had sex with a man.

And my relationship with Paige only slightly enhanced my understanding of capital-S sex. I meant what I said to Sarah—we did stuff, but you may recall that our communication on tough subjects was a little weak.[18]

Everything felt normal when I was with her, when there was no one in the room to make us feel gay. After we kissed for the first time, we progressed in a steady manner toward PG-13 content.

But if there was no one in the room to make us *feel* gay, there was also no one in the room to teach us how to *execute* gay. I am using *italics* to insinuate that I am talking about *sex*.

Since I didn't learn much about what sexual pleasure means to women, it logically follows that I knew even less about how two women pleasure each other; but it is my firm belief that, like a room full of monkeys destined to type out *Hamlet*, two people attracted to one another will be able to intuit any number of cinematic sex scenes.

Eventually, only one final frontier remained before Paige and me. An act whose Webster's moniker sounds as fleshy and outlandish as the act itself, which I can barely spell for you now—so primal that it retains its deep heritage of nineteenth-century Latin origins. A word that so literally describes the action, spelling out instruction, that its redundancy should negate any necessity on my part to actually commit to writing it in a public forum. And while an act of oral sex performed on a man gets any number of easily spouted nicknames—*blowy, blowjob, job, head, suckin' dick, deep-throatin'*, even *licking like a lollipop*, if you're Lil Wayne—I have, for the last one hundred words, tried to put off the inevitable moment when I must type that

---

[18] :/

word that starts with a *C* and ends with *unnilingus*. Over the course of eighteen months, I had feared this moment most of all.

Then it happened. Her, taking the approach of a turtle tasting a dipping sauce, and then later, me, pursuing the technique of a fish intaking water. Both wrong.

As I lay down next to her—looking, as one does, at the ceiling—I asked, "So that was s-sex for us, right?"

And she replied, "I mean, we've been having sex this whole time." Already embarrassed that I had asked if we had just had sex for the first time, I didn't dare find out more. So I had no idea where I stood on sex, pleasure, or even desire.

Which is how I wound up, many years later, discovering that my virginity had slipped through the cracks somewhere along the way.

And yet, like the hairy-toed Bilbo that I am, some part of me wanted to cling tightly to my virginity. To keep *precious* safe.

If virginity is something that slips through the cracks, then how could I be sure that I had waited for the right person? If sex is more akin to a joined arousal, then I have no idea where, when, or how I had my first sexual encounter. That pretty much makes me a whore.

I use *whore* in the way that Hannah Gadsby does in her Netflix special *Nanette*—as the opposition to *virgin*. Women have historically faced the choice between being a virgin or being branded a whore—essentially a categorization that serves to determine who is worthy of our respect and who is not.

Virginity is an abstraction, and it's an abstraction that benefits men. It benefits men with filthy records who desire women with purer ones, like dogs marking territories.

I had recklessly pitted myself against whores to assure myself that I was on the "right" track. The more we dwell on who is and is not a virgin, or what women do with their bodies, the more we hold women back. So, we must ask ourselves, who benefits from fracturing our gender into competing camps? Now that I'm a whore I'll tell you—not we.

I'm much older now than when I wet the bed, and in all the times I've tried to distance myself from other women, I didn't realize that, in addition to mischaracterizing women at large, I was also doing myself a great disservice to myself, for trying to hold on to some vision of myself as tame. I wanted to want to be good. But every time I thought about what a good girl would do, I somehow got lost on my way to following suit.

At the end of the day, I'm the fool for thinking I wasn't supposed to *want*.

At least *want* as it is synonymous with craving, desire—dreaming, even. I think I clung so tightly to the idea that I was a virgin because it was one of the last tendons that bound me to a possible goodness when, in so many other ways, I had failed. I couldn't socialize right, I couldn't dress right, and, with the added realization that I was gay, I couldn't love right.

In the years after coming out, even as I conceded that I could never be her, I never stopped comparing myself to the perfect girl.

Who is the perfect girl? She is elusive yet everywhere—everything all at once. She is smoke-like by design, filling any vessel, yet impossible to capture. You know who she is—or at least, you feel who she is—but if we tried to describe her in more perfect detail, you would lose sight of her form in your mind's eye.

*Because if she is everything at once, then in fact, she must also be nothing at any particular moment. A mere vehicle for the virtue of the day.*

"Socially compliant," "nice," "cooperative." These are among the most commonly unearthed qualities that we, as a social group at large, value in women.[19] The best way to be a woman, it would appear, is to not *be* at all, since all three of these descriptors require someone else's needs to assert themselves first. And acquiescing is an all but required part of the social order—in Kate Manne's book, *Down Girl*, she talks about misogyny (from all genders) as the psychological punishment we assign to women who fail to do just that. "What could be a more natural basis for hostility and aggression than defection from the role of an attentive, loving subordinate?"

We can't really be free if our only choices in life are safety or danger; freedom lies somewhere in between, I think.

This book wasn't really supposed to be about womanhood with a capital W.

To understand the challenge of defecting from my social identity as a straight, cisgender woman—my *peerness*, you need to know that I was raised on a cautionary tales of women who have labels as all "unbecoming women—traitors to the cause,

*Psst*

*PSSST*

sorry, will you give me a moment?

What?!

---

19  See *Social Psychology of Gender*.

THREE WELL-EDUCATED WOMEN walk into a bar and sit down at a table—a future doctor of internal medicine, a future doctor of physical therapy, and a future person of unspecified employment (me). A little-known variation on a classic. We were catching up after living as college graduates for at least two years. I remarked to myself how much more grounded we seemed, now that our worlds had grown beyond dorm rooms and frat parties.†

Two men pulled up chairs next to us, almost in unison, implying a premeditated and strategic strike. They surrounded us from two sides. I was annoyed—resentful that they thought they could simply join our table without invitation—and I briefly, shamefully, lamented that picking straight people up at a bar was about as easy as sitting down at a table with your back to the world.

These men were drunk, and not on German pretzels with Sriracha dipping sauce. They were drunk drunk. And they were big. Big big. The man to my left, the brains of the operation, as would soon be apparent, wore army-print pants, in uniform as a man ready for combat. He was also the bigger of these two men. When they initially tried to speak to us, I played deflector. As a gay woman, I have acquired quick bar banter that cuts men loose before they can get my name. In response to their drunken

---

† This particular alcohol establishment serves excellent bar bites of various international descent. My roommate and I have, on more than one occasion, gotten sick from overindulging and mixing—not our alcohols, but our finger foods. Lamb sliders with chimichurri just don't quite sit with pâté bánh mì

prattling, I cut to the chase. "We're just here to hang out. Would you mind kindly leaving us in peace?" That this unapologetic rejection didn't deter them, that it didn't leave them mortified, marks a severe chasm between how we raise men and women.

These men were more determined than ever. My defenses were firing. "We're actually all gay." I didn't ask my straight friends for their permission before taking them under my protective gay wing—the safe space where a bar is just a place to buy alcohol, not a chessboard of drawn-out gamesmanship. "I don't care if you are lesbians," he said. Maybe he meant that he just wanted to get to know us and enjoy our company. But I doubted it. To me, the implication was that our sexual preferences mattered little to him, our desires an afterthought. Meanwhile, his companion—so good at following military direction, not so good at speaking in coherent sentences—was remarking on the cilantro garnishing my sesame udon noodle salad. He grabbed a handful and shoved it into his mouth, insightfully noting that "this spinach tastes weird." He chewed with his mouth open as little pieces lodged themselves in between his oversized teeth.

In the next two or three exchanges between the big man and me, my friends growing increasingly quiet and downcast, I explicitly informed him that they had intruded and respectfully requested that they leave us alone. His answer was still no, and his friend still chomped on cilantro.

So, here was our dilemma, an emblematic microcosm of women's experiences, our choices were thus: give in and let them sit at our table while we sat in silence; fight them, which—despite my thorough dedication to exclusively watching women's sports on television in pointed appreciation for their athletic talent—I had to admit would end poorly; or begin to hurl insults, preparing ourselves for a deluge of commentary about our unkindness. My preference would be none of those things; my preference would be to say, "I'll let you know if I'd like to talk to you."

At some point, they finally left. We had settled for option A, in which we all sat in silence, and they were eventually uncomfortable enough to leave. But the big man came back. "Sorry we bothered you. We're bad people. I apologize for my behavior." I thanked him. I told him that I appreciated his apology. "No, you're not a bad person, but no, you're still not welcome at our table." I felt thankful that, as a gay woman, it wasn't so refreshing to find an apologetic and sincere man that I might have felt compelled to take my pants off on the spot.

But the big man was mad again. He asked me what I did with my life. I said I was getting my PhD. This was not explicitly true, but at this time in my life I was tasting how that felt coming out of my mouth. Additionally, for this particular encounter, I wanted as much in my arsenal as possible; I felt compelled to add educational prestige to feel validated as an expert in what I wanted and could ask of this scenario.

He asked me if that was all. Thinking he meant one thing, I added a couple of hobbies to my list of occupations. He meant the other thing. He meant, is that all I do with my life, that fragile thing between birth and death that we all risk wasting. He whipped his phone out. He was a military man, he said, but I was seeing neither pictures of the military nor pictures of the man. Instead, I was seeing pictures of guns. He was letting me know just how dangerous he could be. He was showing me the violence he could enact. "I risk my life every day for your freedom," he said—though clearly not my freedom to pick my tablemates, or, for that matter, my freedom to shove my own damn cilantro garnish into my own damn mouth. He fought for my freedom but resented me for making a choice that didn't include him. My freedom was conditional.

I suppose he wanted my gratitude but probably didn't understand that bravery and courage aren't supposed to be transactional—that it undermines the words' very meanings. He was angry that I didn't treat him more reverently, despite the fact that my very first iteration of "get the fuck away from us," was firm, yet respectful. Which is why, when he implied that I lacked human decency, I was dumbfounded, for that was exactly what I had given him approximately twenty minutes earlier in the evening. It was almost as if, and bear with me, he didn't care about having my respect at all and was after something else.

He left again, performing the same ritual of grabbing Cilantro Sam and saying, "Come on, they clearly don't want us here." (It simply couldn't have been clearer). But one more time he came back (despite how very clear it was). "You're a real jerk," he told me. "We just got back, and my buddy is having a hard time." In an attempt to tap into my feminine duty—soothing the soul of a troubled man with an abundance of nurturing—the big man had unwittingly summed up my role in a capitalistic, patriarchal society. He performed his role as the laser-focused, mission-driven, self-sacrificing army man, and I was supposed to comply, entrusted to provide care and comfort for his buddy's emotional homecoming. The blunt subtext was that in exchange for benefitting from his body in combat, I owed his friend mine.

For all the rhetoric that women are too emotional to make level-headed decisions, I knew that only a man could afford to blow up in rage at an unwanted visitor—a release I deeply craved but knew I could never have. I had to be assertive, but I couldn't be a jerk; I had to be kind, but I couldn't be seen as too inviting. I needed to state my case, but given his size, my size, his military training, and my snarky mouth, I had to handle this situation calmly and carefully. If I ran, he might have followed; if I shouted, he might have struck. It was safest to stand still, making imperceptible movements toward my safety, using only the armament of deliberate vernacular.

It was recognizing this subtext that allowed me to be firm in my response: no. Which inspired him to ask me one final question: "Do you get off on shitting on veterans?" Naturally, if I wasn't sexually aroused by his very presence, I must be somehow sexually aroused in my refusal. Either way, his narrative sexualized me. I had attempted to diminish my role in this man's life. He—and only he—had decided to make me a person of interest.

And we're supposed to want this, right? To be objects of attraction? Our Victorian model of courtship means that women are expected do our best to seduce, to become sex objects. Of course, we've made strides—we can lean in now, if we want to. But it is so infinitely clear that our new-found agency is conditional—that we should still strive to be likable, compliant, and passive. We have choices, but we still face punishment for failing to make the "right" ones. And despite learning that attracting men wouldn't bring me any fulfillment, it seemed that I would never actually have the choice to opt out of being the object of a man's desire.

There, in that bar, a woman who never wanted to kiss a man (ever, ever) again still had to fight tooth and nail to prove that she did not. On paper we have freedom, but the tyranny remains in all the ways in which our social order punishes deviants and leaves those who continue to resist without a roadmap on how to move forward. It can sometimes feel futile, even, to continue to assert our humanity when we feel those social strictures tightening around us. And yet, for those of us who desire to feel fully and unconditionally free, we have no choice but to keep trudging.

He left one final time—whether it was because his larger group collected him and his fellow soldier or because the bartender shooed him to the street outside, I don't recall. I watched intently as he was loaded into the back of a truck, which he only conceded to after attempting to declare himself the driver. I made sure his body had gotten into the vehicle that was driving away from me, his threat dissipating with the emissions of his tail pipe. The bartender came up and offered a nonchalant apology. I asked him, facetiously yet pointedly, if he had seen our cries for help. I wanted to make it clear that this was a potentially dangerous situation—one that he should look out for in the future. He apologized again, offering us free drinks. Under other circumstances, I would have declined, hoping to seem easy going rather than demanding (and yes, those drinks could have been seen as payment to placate me or to silence any complaints I could have about that bar), but I decided to say yes to a round on the house—partly because I didn't want to say the words, "It was no problem," and partly because I needed a reason to stay at the bar for another thirty minutes to make sure the white truck wasn't lurking nearby to follow us home.

So we sipped, my sour beer tasting extra sour as I accepted a reward for a race I had never wanted to run. We tried to make light of what had just happened, grateful that we had a man with a mouthful of cilantro on whom we could focus our bewildered memories. We laughed because we had to, because we were at a bar with friends, because we weren't ready to discuss the tireless and familiar frustration of that encounter.

This book wasn't really supposed to be about womanhood with a capital W.

But to understand the challenge of defecting from my preordained social identity as a straight, cisgender woman, in order to live out my queerness, you need to know that I was constantly inundated with cautionary tales of women who have failed: what Manne might call "*unbecoming* women—traitors to the cause of gender—bad women, and 'wayward' ones."

My mother was often telling me to "be a lady" or to "grow up." This is not bad advice—by which I mean, it's not lacking in love or affection. She was trying to point me toward safety, toward *becoming* my final form: a woman. She was merely reminding me that I was off course, or behind schedule, or just doing *it* wrong.

But the truth was that since I took off to New York—to live alone, to be *singular*—I've been un-becoming a woman. I've been looking more and more like Fred.

*Who is Fred?!* The people are clamoring for an explanation.

The summer I turned eleven, I spent the first week of vacation with a friend at a ranch in Montana. Being a little shy, I hadn't said much up to that point in the trip. The de facto ranch hand was driving us around in the back of a truck when he turned to me and said, "What's your name again? Fred?"

Well, of course it was. I settled into the name as I slouched into the side of a truck bed, elbows propped wide. Embodying Fred was as easy as adjusting my posture and relaxing my shoulders—all that was missing was a long reed of canary grass and maybe a cowboy hat I could angle higher off my face with my pointer finger.

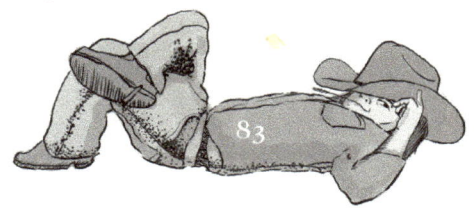

Later that summer, I went to my very first sleepaway camp off the coast of Washington. Again, I was a little nervous to be with strangers, and before I knew it, I was introducing myself to bunkmates as Fred: "My name is Annie, but you can call me Fred," as if that were a perfectly reasonable nickname. I don't know what Annie did at camp, but Fred made a name for herself. In the cafeteria, Fred wagered with fellow campers that she would be able to finish an entire second helping of super-nachos *and* lick the plate clean.

At home, my mother prescribed for us a chic sensibility that did not include plate-licking. Again, the rules of womanhood. Fred did not give a shit about those rules. Fred was free to make the choices (and mistakes) she needed to make—some mistakes that were obvious only seconds after squeegeeing an enamel camp plate clean with her tongue.

What a hoot.

At the next summer camp I went to, I didn't even think twice before introducing myself as Fred—because Fred meant a freedom from weighing normalcy against the things I wanted to do, make, and be.

Fred liked the things she liked. When many kids chose lake time for their elective hour, Fred went to the camp coffee house to drink hot chocolate and appreciate the finer complexities of *Harry Potter and the Half-Blood Prince*. When campers chose to pursue horseback riding, Fred went to the craft shed and built a shoe rack. It was nothing special, this shoe rack—unfinished wood, wobbly joints—but she needed a shelf for her cabin, and Fred went from idea to actualization without giving things a second thought, particularly on whether or not this was the "right" way to do camp.

Much like my shoe rack, which was immediately disposed of, Fred was abandoned upon my arrival back home. She didn't belong in my world.

Fred: the ultimate wayward woman; a lost (tom)boy who never grew up.

Ironically, I think she might just be the pillar of wisdom I should have looked to as I was coming to terms with my identity—as a lesbian, as a writer, as a genderqueer wayward someone.

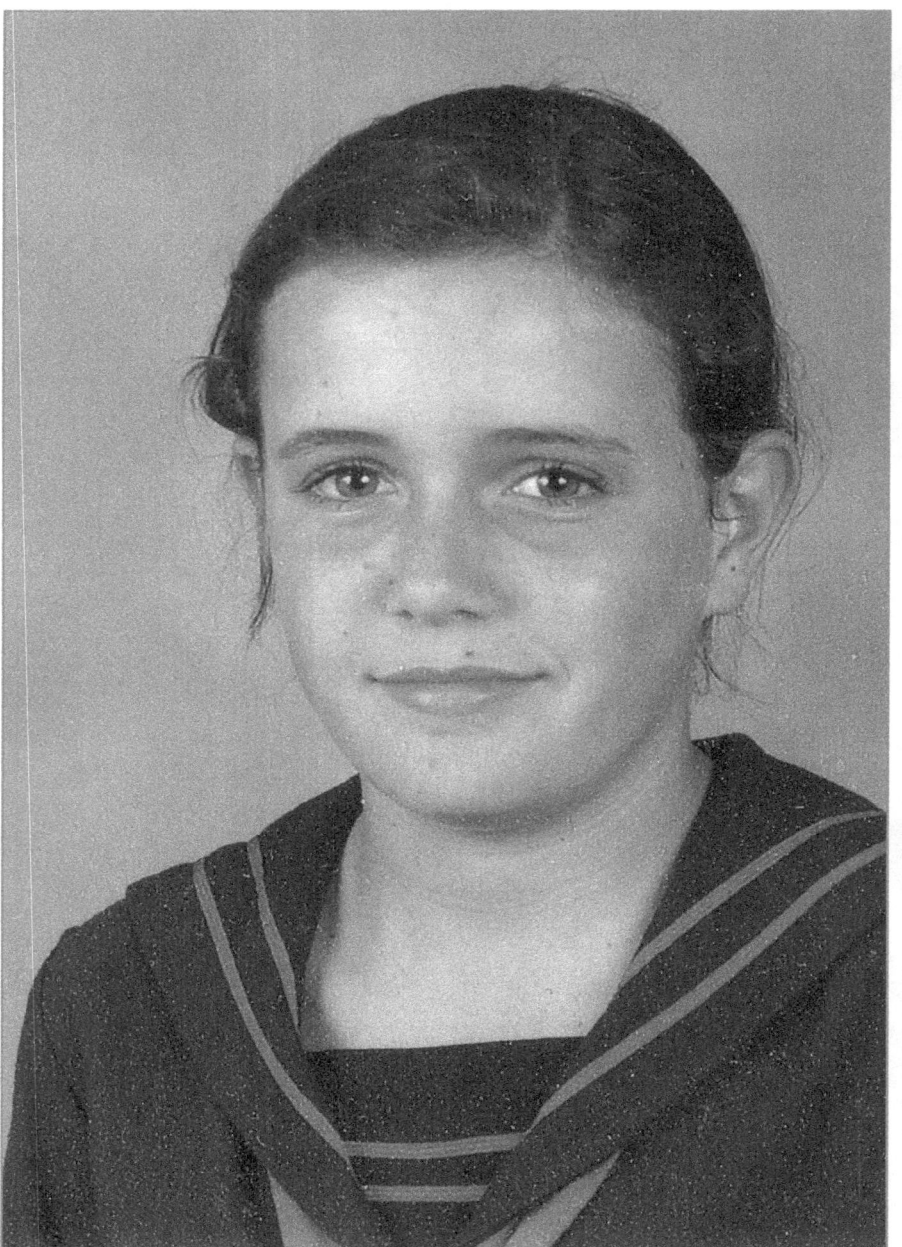

2007-08

Annie Krabbenschmidt

# A Movie Review

2018 was a banner year for queers in film—a fact upon which *The Atlantic*'s Spencer Kornhaber has already dutifully reported. While we've seen queer people portrayed in movies before, in major roles even (think *Milk*, *Brokeback Mountain*, *Transamerica*), what this year's movies have in common, as Kornhaber notes, is that they focus on coming out and the declaring of one's adolescent self.

This storyline has been much awaited. Even the most queer-centric films of the past have presented queer characters in a state of being that is taken for granted, encouraging audiences to see queerness as a binary of existence or non-existence: there are gay people in the world and here they are. For liberal audiences, this characterization is an opportunity to declare sympathetic allegiance to the marginalized.

In the presence of more sidelined roles, this is an opportunity for stereotyping and segregation. Growing up, many movies and television shows I watched depicted the insidiousness of lesbianism as a threat. Typically, this was in the form of a character who, for the purposes of slap comedy, often presented her sexuality with such brazen confidence that one might mistake her for a straight white man. I assumed that queer people were so self-possessed that they simply came into being.

Alternatively, lesbianism appeared as a form of punishment for failing to be the right kind of woman. Liz Lemon is appalled that Jack Donaghy set her up on a date with his female friend; he explains his assumption of her sexuality by pointing to her sneakers that are "definitely bi-curious." That was how the media depicted sexuality before I was ready to accept my own queerness. No wonder it took me so long to say those words aloud.

What 2018's films have done well is present gay people in a state of change that almost all queer people have had to confront (if not in action, then at least in contemplation): coming out of the closet.

While no one should make the mistake of believing that coming out of the closet or acting on sexuality is about "becoming gay," the experience is a becoming of sorts. "Coming out of the closet" is a transitory descriptor for a reason, and the journey has hurdles that even the most sympathetic of straight people cannot imagine. Kornhaber's astute thesis is that queer coming-of-age films depict the ultimate challenge—deciding to pursue a life that bears no resemblance to those of friends, family, and most peers and mentors. Queer characters are therefore inherently and genuinely rebellious—not merely in the way they appear to be in films like *The Breakfast Club*: rebellious, but ultimately pre-adults destined for the same future as their parents.

The genre of queer films of the past has therefore neglected the one triumphant story we have desperately needed—the coming out movie.

In my own personal narrative, I gazed unto a sea of Duke fraternity brothers and wondered if it was the sweat glistening from their exposed, unevenly hairy chests that turned me off, or their gender (a very close call that was ultimately decided in favor of gender). With no outlet in which to discuss the challenge that lay ahead of me, I began scripting parts of a movie that would eventually serve as my declaration; my movie poster was to say, "A Coming ~~of Age~~ Out Film."

It was to my great disappointment that *Love, Simon* portrayed much the same scenery that I had plotted—the liberal enclave that somehow isn't liberal enough, the father's seemingly innocuous gay jokes, and the portrayal of gay people as harmlessly "just like us" (even gay men do sports!). On the last narrative element, I had particularly great concern as a teen.

When I began presenting my script idea to my film studies capstone class back in 2014—under the guise of being a straight person interested in the topic—my film teacher suggested I present my character staring longingly at soccer teammates' bodies. My heart thudded as I nervously told him that "it doesn't work that way."

Despite the warm and fuzzies that *Love, Simon* brings me (with only a little resentment that someone beat me to making this movie), the movie doesn't adequately address the muddiness that accompanies understanding oneself. Instead, it is about the challenge of proudly stating what he already knew. *Boy Erased* also fails in this regard. How can a boy, indoctrinated by anti-gay religious beliefs his entire life, state matter-of-factly to his god-fearing parents that he is gay when I, a child of San Francisco, could not?

Of course, an added issue in *Boy Erased* is that the movie centers so much on the horrors of conversation therapy that the program nearly takes on the role of main character. While this movie undoubtedly serves an activist purpose, drawing our attention to a very real occurrence in modern day America, a story of this nature encourages the audience to channel their emotions into outrage against some "backwards" parts of the world rather than to understand the overarching challenges of being gay in any city.

In truth, the questions "What do I want?" "What do I like?" and "Who even am I?" plagued me, and, even after six years of being proudly out of the closet, they still do. For this reason, I would like to make the case that only one film gets it right—the indie darling, *The Miseducation of Cameron Post*, directed by Desiree Akhavan and starring Chloë Grace Moretz, which is based on a book of the same name—a book which queer women have been passing to each other in secret for years. In the movie, our protagonist, Cameron, falls in love with her best friend, Coley, and then is sent to "God's Promise," a treatment camp for those that suffer from Same Sex Attraction (SSA).

My bias should be immediately obvious—this is a story about queer women in a sea of films about queer men (which, in turn, float in a sea of films about straight men); but even so, this movie tapped into a facet of queerness that most films misrepresent and most straight people gravely misunderstand: the confusion.

My god, so much confusion.

For starters, there's the blurry distinction between close friendship and romance, which forces you to ask the question, "Do I love her like a sister or love her like a girlfriend?" In high school, some straight girls held hands; in college, some straight girls made out. Some of us FaceTime our best friends for two hours; some of us still have sleepovers. Then there's the fact that, for some gay people, exploring sexuality begins as an attraction to personalities, leaving the physicality of romance for much, much (muuuuuch) later. Closely aligned is the prospect of falling in love with one specific person, leaving us, when that one person ultimately decides to stomp on our young gay hearts, to wonder if there will be other women we could love.

And of course, tightly weaving these questions together is the presence of neurological work that is beyond our control. It is nearly impossible to explain repression to someone who has never experienced it— how all at once, you can have one hundred percent clarity on a dilemma you didn't even dare debate at the conscious level.

*Cameron Post* is such a relief because it depicts our queer heroine approaching her sexuality timidly, not just with the outside world, but in her own self-understanding. A world in which conversion therapy exists as a possibility is certainly a stark contrast to the liberal haven experienced by urbanites like me, but in *Cameron Post*, it's almost as if questions of faith and the institution of Christianity stand as proxy for understanding our place in the social order. One can easily swap god's intention with Adam Smith's invisible hand. For all the education attained by the liberal elite, we don't readily identify capitalism's popular culture machine as such a forceful social institution. Our mantras delineating normal from abnormal are so internalized that we can call them to mind as quickly as a preacher can draw from bible verses.

Confronting a marginalized identity therefore takes an incredible amount of soul searching that can freeze you in your tracks. Enter Cameron. In the beginning of the movie, she wordlessly falls in love with Coley—an innocuous touching of feet turns into a full-on make out with no discussion. It is only when people find out that the two have been intimate that Cameron has to start finding words to understand herself. And of course, Coley abandons her, leaving her to figure out her sexuality as a matter of the self, not of the pair. It is a member of her group at God's Promise who first presents to her the idea of SSA.

Throughout the movie, Cameron confronts questions of her past and present with reticence that her peers mistake for recalcitrance. The reality, as cinematically depicted through Cameron's searching eyes and frequent flashbacks, is that she does not yet have answers. God's Promise does not have the double doors and tight security present in *Boy Erased*—anyone can walk away into the woods if they so choose; the question of "and go where?" is easily read as a question of "and be who?" Not everyone stays in the closet because they face actual threats of punishment. Many simply fear the abyss that awaits, having no models or mentors to lead the way. At the end of the film, when she burns a letter from Coley and asserts her worth as a human, she walks away from God's Promise (or, if you will, Adam Smith's Promise).

While this movie gratified me for all the reasons I have overindulgently stated, I would also like to extend an olive branch to people who do not share my specific history: more specifically, "straight" people. When we finally have a film that focuses on questioning identity, we might open a door to more people asking questions of their nuanced selves. At a school like Duke, questioning—either about sexuality or about life's purpose—is a very vulnerable position to be in. How is it that so many eighteen-year-olds can coincidentally stumble upon management consulting as their eventual career?

Exploring sexuality and owning your identity as a sexual being is also a challenge that straight people ought to face, whether they realize it or not. For women in particular, asserting that you have sexual attractions might etch away at the false ties between wanting sex and being slutty. For men, perhaps questioning your manliness would be a much-needed reprieve from asserting it. And for everyone who finds themselves unable to align purely with either gender— free yourself from trying.

And, for selfish reasons, normalizing asking questions of sexuality and identity will alleviate that burden from the shoulders of queer kids, who, fifty years after Stonewall, still have a challenge ahead.

# ACT II

**Anniegram**

 **Annie Krabbenschmidt**
@krabbypatty415

# Coming Out ... Again

  **Coming Out Day 2016**

It would be ignorant to assume that every person can come out to family and friends at this moment. Not everyone has the privilege of a safe space and close confidants. But for those of us that do, our visibility matters. Visibility ensures that for every tokenized, boxed in, stereotypical representation we see of ourselves in the media, we also see someone who is a real, nuanced, and complicated human being, who also happens to be gay.

# Half Windsors & Best Men

WHEN I WAS five, I found out that a mousy-haired boy named Willie Brewer was going to be Spider-Man for Halloween. I decided that I would never again know happiness if I was not also dressed as Spider-Man for Halloween. Unfortunately, my mother had been hard at work on a *101 Dalmatians* costume for the family.

My sister, Catherine, and I were going to be dalmatians and my dad was to be "Skinner," an oft-forgotten character whose job was to, well, skin the coats of puppies in service of my mother, the fur-crazy Cruella de Vil. I suspect that my mother's love of high fashion, and the thin strip of gray hair that emerged in her early thirties, were the entire reason this family costume came to be.

Not known for her sewing abilities, my mom was using a hot glue gun to adhere black spots to a set of white leggings when I threatened to turn her world upside down with my request. The look of horror on her face was reflective of both the ingratitude I had flaunted and the work it would take for her to find me a Spider-Man costume—namely, stepping foot under the fluorescent lighting of a Target store, which was out of the question.

I attended my kindergarten Halloween celebration demoralized. I was only slightly uplifted when my best friend, Jean, also showed up as a dalmatian; however, her costume was a Disney-official, full-zip suit, undoubtedly purchased at a Spirit Halloween, another storefront that gives my mother hives.

Unfortunately, Jean would not be attending my family's neighborhood Halloween party, which was the main unveiling of our family costume. Tensions were high, since hors d'oeuvres were underway, my dad was late, and what even is a *101 Dalmatians* costume without the beloved Mr. Skinner?

My dad was an accountant, working sixty-to-eighty-hour weeks in San Francisco. I had a general awareness that he was busy and sometimes missed family events, but a lot of the time, he was my pal, teaching me how to throw a baseball, letting me try on his neckties, and showing me how he would shave.

When he finally came home, he picked up a knife and dabbed on some fake blood for a quick family photo shoot. Then he pulled me aside to my bedroom, and I discovered the real reason he was late. He presented a Target shopping bag, and inside was one generic, commercially manufactured Spider-Man suit, with muscular contours that were made of the flimsy foam that never loses the creasing it earns from its packaging.

When I made my subtle entrance into the family room where the party was taking place (read: I pretended that I was swinging from cabinet to counter), my mother scowled at both of us. Cruella indeed.

Costumes have immense power. We communicate ourselves to other people through clothing, sure, but what's more mind-blowing is the way in which clothes have an impact on our relationship with ourselves.

Hajo Adam and Adam D. Galinsky conducted a study at Northwestern University, in which participants wore white coats to take a cognitive test. When the coat was labeled as a "doctor's lab coat," the symbolic meaning of the piece of clothing enhanced attention and performance on the test. The authors refer to the influence that clothing has on psychological processes as "enclothed cognition."

I've never worn a doctor's coat but when I was nine, I dressed as Robin Hood for Halloween. The costume came with a plastic bow and an impotent little arrow with a suction cup at its point. Still, I had an unfamiliar confidence to me, which bordered on needless aggression.

A friend came home from school with me that day and we had disagreed about whether or not to open a window. She was approaching the window as I stood across the room, and in a swift motion that would rival Orlando Bloom's choreographed arrow slinging in *Lord of the Rings*, I whipped that plastic arrow into the square pane of glass that my friend was facing, and yelled "Leave it CLOSED, I SAY!" She slowly turned her head to take in the bright orange plastic rod that was inches from her head and still wobbling into stillness. A perfect shot.

It wouldn't be too much of a leap to say that enclothed cognition, repeated over and over, might lead to a sort of profound confidence. The kind that can't be quantified: the extreme power of feeling neither naked nor clothed—when you feel a perfect alignment between being and dressing and you think for a moment, "Could I possibly *be* this cool?"

This version of myself, the one who suffered from no Freudian lack, wasn't always welcome at home. According to my family, I was beyond incapable of dressing myself.

I wore the same jeans every day of high school. This might not be the end of the world for some, but for my mom, it was like I was communicating to others that I didn't have parents that cared for me. She was so worked up about it that every few months, I would find my jeans balled up in the laundry room, which meant that my mom was getting ready to tell me that they had run away to go to a special farm for good jeans. With one pair of pants, though, it doesn't take long to notice that someone's hidden them from you.

My family may not have understood this, but at times, I cared quite a bit about my appearance and had an eye for unique pieces. My friend, Kelly, and I spent hours watching as vintage Patagonia fleeces went live on eBay. I also had a carefully orchestrated tradition my junior year called Neon Wednesdays, which involved wearing as many loud colors as I could find in my closet. Sometimes, it was just a hat from my sister's sorority events; sometimes, it was madras shorts, a neon-yellow shirt, and a sweatband, all at the same time. But one man's mess is another man's Jackson Pollock. The point is, I thought through these things more than my mom may have realized.

## Annie Krabbenschmidt

And in case she was right—that my clothing would repulse people—I would always bring a dozen bagels to win over unsuspecting classmates on my weekly holiday.

Occasionally, I did wonder if my being single had anything to do with what I wore. Junior year, I had a crush[20] on a boy in the grade above me named Jeff. My friend, Maddie, who had actually dated a boy once, offered to take me shopping—because clothing must have been the reason Jeff and I weren't dating. My mom practically showered Maddie with cash to find me something to wear. We bought a pair of capris, two identical tank tops, and a padded bra. The idea was that I would wear the padded bra *with* the tank top! We called this busty version of me "Annie 2.0." I made it about two days before going back to my jock uniform. Even now, we'll never know if a lack of padding was the reason I never found a good man.

At a small birthday party that year, which Jeff attended, I dressed in an outfit my sister picked out for me. But by the end of the night, when I needed confidence for a round of beer pong, I knew I needed to be wearing the bright pink Patagonia fleece I had tracked down on the internet. Catherine pulled me aside with so much urgency and seriousness that you would think someone had scuffed up a favorite handbag of hers.

Through clenched teeth she said, "*Take. Off. The fleece.*" When I refused, she spent the rest of the night walking behind my friends, gesturing that I take off the fleece, which looked like a drill sergeant being forced to mime a strip tease.

I never buckled. I had no idea that I was gay, but I did think that any man who couldn't love me in a power outfit proba-

---

20  One of those fakies, you know?

bly wasn't meant for me. And while it was true that men didn't come flocking, I mostly felt secure in who I was by the time I graduated high school.

Then came Duke.

Eighteen-year-olds fueled by a fastidiousness that had thus far served them well watched each other like rare English hawks. Everywhere you looked, you could find Tory Burch sandals, Van Cleef necklaces, ironed straight hair, and Barbour jackets—a brand I knew from a 2004 photo shoot in which my entire family wore matching ones. If there was an even slightly queer contingent somewhere on campus, it wasn't easy for me to find in those first few years. And, having lost my status as a varsity athlete, I had very little to show off.

I tried my hardest to fit in, swapping championship sweatshirts for cable knit sweaters. I actually worried about what I was wearing and felt self-conscious about my wardrobe for the first time. For eighteen years, my mom had used all the cruel remarks she could to convince me that I was dressed wrong, and I didn't believe her until that first year of college.

And lest you think that I was simply suffering an identity crisis and being hard on myself, I have a 100% accurate anecdote for you.

I took an acting class my first semester. I had performed some comedy over the summer and found that I quite enjoyed the stage. For reasons I was clearly not privy to knowing during my enrollment period, my Introduction to Acting class was entirely composed of athletes and "general hotties." In case you're like me and didn't know this, some of my classmates—the entire Duke men's basketball freshman class—were something of a big deal.

A month into the semester, our instructor conducted an exercise about judgment. One lucky member of the class would stand in the middle of the circle, and the rest of the class would say the very first assumptions that came to mind. It's the kind of activity that every young girl dreams of enduring her first month of college. Though I was clearly the least popular person in the class, the one who neither played a varsity sport nor was bound for a "key three" sorority, I was selected as our first subject.

As I stepped into the circle, wearing sister-approved clothing, boots, *and* under-eye concealer, the students around me started sizing me up.

"Nerdy."

"Uptight."

"Naïve."

"Librarian."

Like any responsible instructor trying to instill a young adolescent with confidence, Dana interrupted this free association—but only so she could wonder aloud if taking my hair out of its bun would help improve my appeal. While there were disingenuous wolf whistles when I complied, I would say the moment was hardly an ego booster.

I held back tears, even as a fair-haired soccer player—wearing her hair in the same messy bun I had walked in with—got up, and my classmates called her "sporty and fun."

Reinstating Neon Wednesdays was unthinkable, but trying to blend in was apparently not working either. I was already stressed about the fact that I was a newly self-aware lesbian, and now I had to figure out if I could live the rest of my life with my hair in my face.

When I was coming out, I kept trying to grab at normative standards as if to salvage myself and minimize my losses. I wore skirts for the first time in my life because it might make people say, "I had no idea!"

There was a huge shift in my relationship to my own appearance. When I realized that I was a lesbian and not a straight tomboy, I was scared that my clothing just added to my "otherness." After so many years of subliminal messaging that lesbians were a dangerous threat to pool parties and sports teams, I wanted to show everyone that there was a difference between me and gay people at large. I wore precious pearl earrings that felt like a glinting member card to the groups on campus, from which I was very much trying to gain acceptance. I can't speak for Paige but I think I can safely assume that both of us wanted to prove that we weren't threatening. When eventually she told her team about me, they said I was cool—even though, in addition to being a lesbian, I was also a NARP (non-athletic regular person).

I knew that my acceptance was contingent on my ability to stay within the boundaries of cool, whatever that meant to the Duke elite—an understanding that came to a head on one particular occasion, when I told Paige that I was thinking of wearing a red sweatsuit to the men's lacrosse team's annual holiday party, which they hosted for other varsity athletes and, yes, hot people.

"Like Santa Claus. I think that would be silly and fun," I said, holding up a Champion brand set.

Before I could even mention finding a beard to wear, she retorted, "I don't think it would." Having been placed in the center of a judgment aquarium, I don't blame Paige for stressing about what her first girlfriend was wearing to the event of the year. She was doing what she thought would keep her safe, and in most ways, I wanted to do the same. I ended up wearing a red, form-fitting shirt and my pearl earrings.

During the six years in which I completed my undergraduate and master's degrees at Duke, I carried with me the awareness that there was safety in conformity; to stand out in any way was risky. Between the ages of eighteen and twenty-two, I was a watered-down version of myself.

Just as clothing had had a way of betraying me, it was also a key to getting back to myself. To Fred, even. When I was finally, *finally* done with Duke, my mother and I took a graduation trip to Woodstock, Vermont—the most goddamn adorable place I've ever encountered. The town is hard not to love and is easily the closest replica of *Gilmore Girls*'s Stars Hollow that I have come across.

We wandered into a vintage clothing store that sold on consignment. Among the racks was a tweed blazer with a velvety black collar. It was a size eight or ten and the fact that it was too large for me was only emphasized by the pads that hung over my shoulders by at least two inches on each side. But when I put it on, I was struck by a feeling not unlike the one I had when I was dressed as Robin Hood or licked my plate clean for an entire gymnasium of fans. And with that feeling, a vision: me, walking through the streets of New York, with this blazer and a messenger bag—I was writer, according to the way I swooshed by on the sidewalk. My mom tried to stop me from buying the jacket because she thought it made me look homeless. But I couldn't be swayed.

The checkout counter of this store was a glass case of further curiosities. I saw a tiny pocket watch and insisted that I needed this too—to drape from my new lapel, obviously.

"I need that," I said.

"You're not a clown," said my mother, in an attempt to triage my fashion faux pas.

We left the store without the watch, but I had my blazer and a post-graduation plan. Start spreading the news.

"This is my time," I told my mom.

New York is a city with a short-term memory and a whole lot of weirdos, each of which simultaneously causes and necessitates the other. I knew absolutely no one and I could be and wear whatever I wanted.

At the first sign of chill, I wore my blazer. I walked, hurried, to nowhere in particular. I walked in the center of the cobblestoned streets of the West Village; I walked with my hands dug in my pockets, using them to open my jacket to a gentle cape; I walked and I soared.

One day, I was on the phone with a friend, catching her up on all that whooshing and soaring. I proposed that I might like to wear a suit to an upcoming wedding we were to attend. Having spent about a month in my tweed blazer, two summers as Fred, and one Halloween night as Peter Parker, I felt ready for this next step. My daily wear had turned to pants with more regularity, and when work required it, I would wear an oxford-style button-down shirt.

But if there was ever a time to dress "right," it would be at a fancy wedding—the perfect intersection of class, etiquette, manners, and hetero pairings. Add to the formality the fact that weddings are often heavily documented—and thus, immortalized—and it's not a good time to look like a fool. Add to *that* the fact that holy matrimony incites a sort of reflection on your desirability, and you've got a real test of will on your hands.

When you are so immersed in the rules of femininity, there is a muddling of the difference between wearing what you want and wearing what you should.

Despite all the years when I had marched to the beat of my own shoe-rack-building hammer, I wore dresses when I had to. At prom, for example, wearing a dress had made me happy because people told me I looked gorgeous, and at seventeen, that was the only word I knew for *desirable*. Still, the happiness was undermined by a feeling that was a little bit like resignation; I didn't feel like myself but accepted that perhaps that was the price of being beautiful.

There were bare legs that needed shaving and thongs that needed wearing and I smiled for photographs and laughed with friends, but I felt weird, like I was just so exposed. Like my limbs were sticking out of my body at odd angles. And I would cross my arms a lot, or grab at my elbows to try and hide myself from the world.

Even with this feeling in my memory, I *knew* what dresses were like. I had no idea what a suit would be like. The devil you know, you know?

I decided that if I was going to wear a suit, I needed to *nail* it. I needed to be the Simone Biles of suit-wearing—the Olympic-level pressure was on. I researched bespoke suiting, particularly companies that specialized in queer tailoring, and I made an appointment at a place in Brooklyn called Bindle & Keep.

In the months before my fitting appointment, I met Stephanie through a friend. When we went on a date a few weeks later, I wore an(other) oversized jacket, a quilted denim number that my mother had called a "tire-changing outfit."

We had the kind of first date that makes you realize that every other date you've been on was trash. On previous first dates, I had made the assumption that merely being able to sit on a bar stool meant you were having a good time; on my first date with Stephanie, I wanted to make that barstool my home. Time was immaterial.

At the end of our date, when Stephanie said that she'd had a good time, her body turning fully toward me, something occurred to me that I had previously refused to believe possible, which was that I knew with certainty that I wanted to kiss someone and that this was the right time to do so. In my tire-changing jacket, I leaned toward her, and our mouths joined together like we had known all along which order to stack our lips—who would come from the bottom and who would come from the top. It was nice. I was ready for nice.

A couple days later, I told her that I would be in her neck of the woods. When she asked what I was doing there, I dodged the question and simply told her I was going to a tailor. When she pushed me, I finally came clean in an apologetic text.

"I'm getting a suit made. Just something I'm trying out."

She told me that she needed a minute to collect herself. And just as I was drafting a few panicky texts about how this would just be a one-time experiment, she followed up that she found women in suits incredibly hot.

And the moment from which she had needed to collect herself was her being turned on.

I was unearthing the possibility that comfort could coincide with attractiveness—that dressing in a way that connected with my core wasn't an inherently horrible style choice.

That had never once occurred to me before.

When I went to my fitting appointment, I had my eyes opened yet again. I brought in pictures of suits that I liked, as well as a picture of me in a baggy, oversized suit that I had tried on at a store. I told Carlos that, despite what my woman's body would have him believe, I didn't want it to look like I was wearing a woman's suit.

"Janelle Monáe looks amazing in her suits, but I don't want to look like that."

Of course, Carlos agreed, I had an androgynous and athletic style: "It's a great style."

My brain briefly short-circuited as I went to contradict him; I had far too many anecdotes in which I had been assured by *literally* everyone that this was not the case, including former acting classmate and pro basketballer Austin Rivers.

An infinity of earth-shattering things happened during that fitting. The first was that I noticed that the tailors were referring to me using they/them pronouns. I hadn't asked them to do so, but there was also no information about my gender on any of my forms. At the time, I believed this was a silent revolution for my non-binary friends, and a demonstration of the uncoupling of gender and appearance. But I didn't realize that maybe it was a liberation for me as well; I didn't *have* to be a "she."

"The thing about a tailored suit," Carlos told me, "is that when it fits you perfectly, it doesn't look like a men's suit or a women's suit. It just looks like *your* suit." It was a simple but profound credo. And it was much like gender, which, without limitations imposed from outside enforcers, could simply be "yours" when pinpointed in an ongoing continuum.[21]

As Carlos wrapped his tape measure under my crotch, I found myself tearing up. How rare it is for women-ish folks like me to have objects made for our bodies, rather than forcing ourselves into sizes and styles that preexist us.

A lot happened between my fitting and the wedding. Stephanie broke up with me quite suddenly, after a month and a half

---

[21] This wisdom comes from my good friend Miranda, who deserves to have their name printed alongside mine as a co-author of this book. See acknowledgements.

of telling me that she wanted to introduce me to her parents.[22] But her sudden choice didn't take away from what I had learned. Stephanie and I had a courtship that changed me in a manner that was altogether different from the way my relationship with Paige had. I was freer, more honest. I gained the incredible knowledge that I, even in a hypothetical suit, was desirable. I was sad when she ended things, but I survived.

A couple days afterward, I started work at a nonprofit serving queer youth, where most of my coworkers were queer. When my queer identity was detokenized, I could finally stop thinking of myself as a lesbian first and a person second. There were rooms full of people I wasn't expected to be attracted to (in fact, this kind of thing is considered inappropriate behavior for a workplace), and there were people with such different interests that I found I was the only freak obsessed with women's professional soccer, something I was sure was one of those genetic traits of being gay. Being able to appreciate variation among us—in our interests, in our qualities, in our flaws—must be how straight people feel every day.

I learned a lot about myself. I learned that I was even less interested in the art of money-making than other queers. I learned that dressing boyishly on a day-to-day basis was not an assured part of being a queer woman. I learned to appreciate

---

[22] Stephanie, on more than one occasion, told me that my pancake recipe was so good that she would never break up with me. It is out of spite—and an inability to ever trust again—that I will not be sharing my pancake recipe in this book.

the fact that I was generally sensitive and warm and that some queer people were not.[23] Perhaps most importantly, I learned that all this was okay. And I, as a person, was okay.

Working at the organization unfortunately spoiled my plans to premiere suited Annie at the wedding. There was a high-profile gala which we were to attend in formal dress. My perfect suit was not ready, but as a happy coincidence, I stumbled upon a nearly perfect—as in, one simple alteration short of perfect—navy-blue suit at a store across the street from my apartment.

On the night of the gala, I nervously dressed in the venue's single-occupancy restroom. Looking in the mirror, I panicked, wishing that I had brought a backup dress to wear in the event that I suddenly found myself panicking in a bathroom. I was seeing my face, but it was like a head attached to someone else's body. I sheepishly poked my head out of the bathroom to tie my tie in the common area where our volunteers were gathering. A delightful member of our marketing team, Diana, caught me as I was making finishing touches.

"Damn," she said with the confidence only someone in marketing can have.

"Really?" I insisted.

"You look hot. Yeah, damn, you look hot. Amazing. And don't think I didn't notice that you're walking with a swagger too."

Actually, I *had* kind of noticed. I had my hands shoved in my pockets, as open and relaxed a posture as I've ever had. I caught

---

23  As Carmen Maria Machado writes about fellow queer folks in In the Dream House, "We are humans and we are human: some of us are unkind … some of us are murderers. And it sounds terrible but it is, in fact, freeing … queer does not equal good or pure or right. It is simply a state of being."

my work crush gazing at me in a mirror, and even if she wasn't, even if I made that up, the delusion was an unprecedented gift. As the night went on, my confidence was almost detestable, and I realized why frat boys feel invincible.

By the end of the evening, I was shimmying left and right and using my tongue to chase my cocktail straw around my glass. My tie hung familiarly around my neck, like we had just conquered the night together, and I was sweaty like a disgusting groomsman. And I was happy.

The wedding was still to come. My sister, having downloaded the colors and patterns of my bespoke suit into her internal Catherine software, spit out the answer to our dilemma of the season, which was over what kind of tie I would wear. Being nothing at all like me, she could call to mind the entire Hermès inventory and knew of a signature item called a Twilly. It was a short tie, like a kerchief or the ascot Fred Jones wears in the Scooby-Doo cartoons.

She sent me the link to a Twilly that was a light blue with some peach and yellow patterning. Discovering it was sold out, I texted my sister in a panic at 8:00 a.m. New York time. She responded immediately—5:00 a.m. in Los Angeles.

"Don't worry, my precious popover. I will acquire the Twilly."

When I asked her why she was awake, she responded that she had intuited a fashion emergency. Of course, the truth was that she is prone to insomnia and late-night candy mongering, frequently waking up with melted candy bars on her pillow and cheeks.

But the next day, true to promise, she found the very last "Trees of Song" Twilly, in a color called Blue Pale Rose, at a brick-and-mortar Hermès store on Rodeo Drive.

I brought my leather oxford shoes, my belt, and my Twilly to Bindle & Keep for my final fitting. The celebration of my unveiling was overshadowed by my neck scarf. Tailors of all genders came over to observe that they couldn't have picked a better tie—it was just so perfectly complementary.

"My sister found it for me," I said, thinking how odd it was that Catherine, a one-time enemy of the state of my wardrobe, should turn up here: at this tailor for bodies that don't conform. Shortly after, she told me that she was already picking out the suit she would wear for my eventual wedding. It means something different for her to wear a suit, but we agreed that she would be allowed if she would go as my best man. If you're lucky, one sibling's gender deviance will inspire a domino-like destruction of nuclear family roles.

What straights don't realize is that queer people (and very cool people, like Fred) make it possible for *everyone* to break the rules. They show us that happiness is worth the fear and the fight, whether the battles are big or small.

And yes, unveiling my suit at Amy and Miles's wedding was everything I hoped it would be. I moved, I grooved, I shimmied, I shook. Sunglasses on, sunglasses off, from every angle one looked, I was caught beaming. Miles told me I was the most beautiful girl there, which I knew was untrue because Amy looked like a goddamned angel, but it was the pseudo-sincere validation I needed.

I never wore a dress again.

**Anniegram**

 **Annie Krabbenschmidt**
@krabbypatty415

# Coming Out ... Again?

   **Coming Out Day 2017**

I'm gay for Gal Gadot, I'm gay for Kate McKinnon, but mostly I'm just super gay. Happy coming out day everybody! It really does get better. Now I can OPENLY pine after celebrities who don't know who I am!

# ITC

### I Moved

Before there was Annie's first suit, there was Inner Thigh Clearance, or "ITC." You've met thigh gap, right? The impossible-to-meet gold standard of women's beauty circa the early aughts? I'll wait if you want to go dig out your old *O.C.* boxset.

I became aware of ITC when I was in middle school. My teenaged sister and her A-list high school friends stood in front of her mirror, tilting their pelvises this way and that to see if there was any angle at which they could stand where their two thighs didn't touch. It was like a real-life version of that *Mean Girls* scene, wherein the Plastics take turns listing their faults. My sister and I have always had very different body types, but I wanted what these girls had and decided that ITC was the ultimate sign of beauty.

Now, *before* there was thigh gap, there was me in a bathing suit—my waffly yellow one that had two giant googly eyes sewn onto the fabric at its belly. I could make the black eyes spin around their casings if I undulated hard enough. If I were more dedicated to swim team, I would have gone for something a little more streamlined, but it was nice to have something to blame for finishing last at every meet.

There I stood, one day at age nine, preparing to execute what I'm sure was a completely intentional belly flop, when someone spoke behind me: "Look at those athletic legs." The words came from another mom, whose kids were tall and blond and would both go on to be stars of their Division I sports teams.

I wondered what made my legs look particularly athletic. Even at nine, I was quick to understand that the answer was something like, "big" or "thick." Perhaps this woman could sense that I would one day *be* athletic, but the evidence was meager, unlike my thighs. Still, the point is not whether this was a positive or negative commentary about my stature. The point is that there was commentary and noise. The point is that, even at nine, I was learning that my body existed in the eyes of others—that I would be evaluated—and that there was something about my legs that made them noticeable, and I would notice the noticing.

This wasn't the first time someone had remarked upon my body. We all get sized up. I knew that I was short, I knew I was a bit mole-y, and I knew that I had a "beauty mark" left of center on my upper lip. It's been more than two decades, and I still think about Jared Bellman telling me, in the second grade, that I had a unibrow every time I touch the soft, fuzzy skin between my two eyebrows. Of course, I was bound to find out about my unibrow eventually. My mother certainly seemed less than shocked when I came home to tell her what I had learned about myself, and she was suspiciously quick to present tweezers to me.

Now, I'll admit that, in my childhood, I was indeed a bit of a jock. I was a ten-sport athlete out of the gate. I was not one for actual working out, but I had excellent hand-eye coordination as well as a reckless disregard for my bodily integrity. I have been concussed, I have split open my bottom lip, torn ligaments, and sprained fingers; for six years, I had a recurring turf burn on my left thigh that would frequently reopen, ooze, and adhere my favorite sweatpants to my skin, leaving little tufts of blue in my scabbing wound. My two front teeth are broken; one has a fake nerve, one has a fake tip. And yes, there is a great deal of documentation regarding my varsity heroics in the *Marin Independent Journal*—ever heard of it?

But for god's sake, I didn't want to *look* athletic.

I've been to at least three debutante balls, so I know that "athletic" is a polite euphemism. It's what you call someone who isn't thin. And despite the fact that "athletic" linguistically indicates some sort of talent, I would have traded all the articles about me that graced the sports section of the esteemed *Marin Independent Journal* to be thin. Pretty. Like the girls my sister brought home.

The thing about having a beautiful family, is that I was reminded every day of what I could be if I made different choices. I had all the genes; I was just too lazy to do the things that needed to be done to be truly beautiful. Athletic, yet somehow also lazy. An impossible paradox.

And a false one—I wasn't actually lazy.

I often found myself performing odd feats with my body. My sister had a baby-faced, rosy-cheeked boy named Tim over one day, and in an effort to impress him, I started climbing the backyard lemon tree. When I fell out of that same tree, he was bewildered, horrified even; I didn't mind, because I had a body in action.

I had not quite made the connection between bodies, their choices, and social acceptance. Humor, bravery (I mean, I climbed a tree), showmanship! That's what I thought was worthy of attention. In a sea of matching sweatshirts, who wasn't staring at the girl who could proudly eat eleven slices of pizza in one sitting—devouring entire slices in one mouthful just to point out that I could. And of course, I can still recall a mess hall of campers chanting "Fred! Fred! Fred!" as I licked that plate clean.

I was comfortable in my priorities. Any day that I didn't have sports practice, I would ride the school bus home and eat straight out of a quart-sized tub of Breyers mint chip ice cream and a family-sized bag of cheddar and sour cream Ruffles while I caught the 4:00 p.m. showing of, yes, *Gilmore Girls*.

But then I went from my K-8 grade school, with the same twenty-nine goony kids I had known since I was five, to the high school my sister and those girls attended. Suddenly, no one seemed interested in how much I could stuff my mouth.

With pizza, I mean!

No one really cared that I was absolutely hysterical either. On the first day of school, I had to wear a shirt my senior buddy had made for me. It had crabs glued all over it, and I'm pretty sure it said "got crabs" on the back—because, you know, Krabbenschmidt. When people asked why, I told them I'd had a bad case in the seventh grade, which was supposed to be hilariously ironic. Not one person found that funny.

I knew some seniors, though, because they had been to my house over the last few years. Now that I was walking their halls, it occurred to me that I should be like them, instead of like me. And they had been silently passing me advice for the last three years. Like that time one of them pantsed me when I was twelve and then started making fun of big bushes? They were talking about me! That was my bush they were talking about! Bushes were bad, it turned out. I was bad.

But, by the end of freshman year, I had learned everything about what made someone cool. With my eye on the prize—coveted invitations to beach parties and boat trips with girls who knew how to carry vodka in water bottles and weed in their bras—I changed.

I was starting to gain athletic status by lettering in two sports (tennis and soccer, thank you so much for asking), and the first obvious step toward desirability was to start practicing harder. The summer after my freshman year, I was playing tennis for two hours every day, hoping to get a promotion from doubles to singles (yes I did, again, thank you so much for asking). It was the first time I had ever really dedicated time to a sport that wasn't part of a mandated practice.

At the tennis court one day, a mother—the same mother, actually, who had called me athletic—caught me after practice. She told me that I looked incredible. What was my secret, she wanted to know.

I told her, "I'm working out more," absolutely beaming. "And," I added, "I'm eating fewer chips."

Because that was the truth. I had stopped snacking.

In high school, fun was fitting in. So in addition to cutting out snacks, I cut out food generally. I got so small so fast that the guidance counselor called me in to see her. For two months, I didn't eat. I was unhappy and I was tired.

And even at my smallest, I never felt thin. Pushing food around my lunch plate, telling my friends that I was eating dinner at home and telling my parents I ate with friends, I knew I was not thin. And even as I incorporated eyeliner into my personal style, I knew I was not pretty. I knew I was not thin because I could immediately collect in handfuls the flesh of my body that separated me from skinniness. I knew I was not pretty because I could identify with certainty the moles, pimples, and hairs on my face and body that separated me from beauty. And there was always more that I could do.

More, more, more, to be less and less and less.

As Jia Tolentino would say in her essay on the topic, I was trying to optimize. Yet, even when my weight was at its lowest, my skin at its clearest, I never felt like I had arrived at beauty. Perfection is a promise that never fails to deliver another promise. And that, I promise *you*, is by design.

But I was, probably in all aspects of my life, optimizing. Isn't that what happens when you spent your infancy at a Yacht Club? Optimizing means only moving forward, never moving back, never pausing, never being at peace. It's a market term, and Tolentino makes it clear that our feelings about bodies and clothing are nothing more than the capitalist impulse in us to mimic the successes of people around us—to try our hardest to be the people we see on magazine covers. The lifestyles of mega rich women, who know how to tells us, without saying a thing, that they are, indeed, mega rich, have become so familiar we mistake them for being ordinary. As Tolentino describes, this person, the ordinary woman, is rewarded for her ordinariness: her professional athlete husband, her four-story brownstone, her extraordinary life, has, through our obsession with celebrity and idealization, become *ordinary*.

I wanted to be ordinary in order to be extraordinary, not knowing that I had chased my tail all the way back to ordinary. In fact, that endless loop *is* what is ordinary. Optimizing. It's tiring. And I wasn't built for that kind of hard work—another failure of mine. What a shame.

Here's how my anorexia ended: a few months into the fall semester of my sophomore year, I nearly fainted onto a friend of mine as I was walking down the library stairs. Then she brought me two slices of pizza, and I ate them to make her proud. And I kept eating because it felt good to have my belly full, and a perfectly ordinary girl had given me the pizza herself.

I quit dieting, which actually had a positive impact on my athletic career. I was strong, and I was a fierce competitor. Being a jock was a core part of my identity; I *am* the hometown guy on the neighboring barstool, recounting the glory days. There's still a YouTube video of me as a young goalie surviving a penalty kick shootout, when I stopped more shots than were scored, which is a very big deal. And I manage to bring that up a lot, because, like I said, it is a very big deal.

I went back to eating for fun, impressing soccer teammates with my ability to eat an In-N-Out 3x3 in (far) less than three minutes. So, I was basically cured.

And yet.

All I had done was figure out how to optimize in a different way. I could spend $x$ less time worrying about food if I spent $y$ time on the tennis court and soccer field, thus maintaining my $z$ sized body (which, at that time, was very tiny). And this was how I stayed small for ten years.

When I went to college, I played club sports, I went to the gym, I discovered rock climbing. I ate salads, I drank lots of water. Like most Duke students, I moved so fast all over campus to optimize the day that I wouldn't have even had time to eat Ruffles and watch television.

While I had never again taken to starvation, I certainly considered my weight almost every day of my life. I argued with myself that I had a healthy relationship with my body—that since rock climbing made me bigger than most girls, and I liked feeling strong, I had somehow overcome hating myself. But lifting my shirt in the mirror and feeling comforted by looking at a well-defined abdomen (less like an egg carton, more like a quilted comforter, but still acceptable) is not a sign of health. After all, the opposite of self-consciousness isn't thinness. The opposite of self-consciousness is, even grammatically speaking, a lack of consideration for whether or not you are thin. Nearly a decade after losing my baby weight, I had never stopped thinking about thinness.

But I assumed that I would just carry on the way I had. Until the day I broke my leg—the day the optimizing stopped.

# Fred

## I Stopped

By the time I was in graduate school, I wasn't really a jock anymore. I had played on a coed soccer league when I lived in San Francisco with Katelin, but it was hard to keep to a schedule as a professional student. I continued rock climbing about three times a week, but few folks in my program knew that about me.

At the end of our first year, however, there was to be a soccer match between my Master of Public Policy program and our sister program, the Masters of International Development Policy. And, being the cliché that I am, I jumped at the chance to captain my team. Just like those high school games under the lights ... rain pouring, minutes left on the clock. Our opponents: the season's unstoppable wall; my defensive line: the immovable force ...

Look, I'm not sensationalizing, that's just what they wrote in the *Marin Independent Journal*.

I digress.

I was elated. Hours before the game, our semester's classes had come to a close, and I was celebrating *play*. There was a warm familiarity to putting on my shin guards and my cleats. At center back, I floated around the field, making epic defensive plays, the likes of which this country hadn't seen since the spring of 2010 ...[24, 25]

---

24  "Saves Her Specialty" was the headline of that particular article in the *Marin Independent Journal*.

25  Okay, but seriously, when I went through *Marin IJ* archives looking for articles, I was expecting some wave of powerful nostalgia to take deep hold of me—instead I discovered that my name was often misspelled, my playing position was once misreported, and I was once listed as a member of the opposing team. Anyway, I have all the articles saved on a flash drive, so just say the word and I'll send them over.

And then, four minutes into the game, I was in the middle of a collision between my goalie and the opposing team's two forwards. There was a twist and a crack and then I was on the ground. One of my athletic legs had shattered. I landed and shouted out so that people would get away from me, and there was a sticky stillness as men on both sides of the game wondered if my crying was "a little much."

The best of people from my class gathered me and my things and took me to the hospital. And to be honest, I didn't feel much of anything at all. Every once in a while, I let out an involuntary groan, maybe just to remind myself that *something* was happening, but adrenaline took care of the rest.

At the hospital, I waited for at least an hour to be seen by someone. When I was finally wheeled back to an exam room, about eight different medical professionals came in and asked me, despite what I thought was very obvious athletic attire, what had happened. How did you fall?

"Gardening accident," I deadpanned.

My mentor and good friend, Adam, once told me that sarcasm didn't suit me. He didn't know that I used to rely heavily on sarcasm to hide from my own hurt. In the hospital, I was hurting. With no self-awareness for my privilege as an able-bodied adult, I was downright insulted that these doctors assumed my body was fragile enough to splinter in any incident that was less than Herculean. And they walked around and didn't seem to care when they were informing me that I would be in a cast for around twelve weeks.

My brain started calculating. It wasn't trying to figure out what to do about the summer internship in New York I was supposed to start in two weeks. Nor was it particularly worried about the finals I had in the coming days.

My brain, god bless it, calculated that twelve weeks was about thirty-six gym sessions that I would miss.

In the ten years since I had decided to be thin, I had never gone more than a week or two without some sort of workout, pushing *something*. For the first time in my life, I was going to be still.

The first days in bed were the hardest. My body, used to motion, kicked around the sheets, trying to squirm out a workout of sorts. I clenched and unclenched my butt cheeks, hoping to keep my hips from getting unruly. When I tired of that, I felt my fat spill out beneath me, like a piece of clay being slowly pushed into a table. When I felt myself pooling a little too far out from my center of mass, I would return to my clenching, trying to grab up parts of me that wanted to expand. Parts of me that, maybe after a traumatic injury, wanted to relax.

The weeks passed, however, and while I watched for my broken leg to grow larger, I instead watched it grow smaller. There remained a rather unflattering assortment of fleshy pockets around my joints, but the shrinking of muscle around my quadriceps was what concerned me the most. Until one day, when I spotted it: ITC.

Even though I had always known that a body like mine wasn't meant to achieve ITC, I also wished I would one day wake up in a different body. But now I had it; I learned for the first time in my life that no amount of activity or dieting would achieve what immobility could. I would have to sacrifice running, climbing, walking—the very use of my body, in order to be one of the girls in my sister's mirror.

## The World Moves

In her book, *What We Don't Talk About When We Talk About Fat*, fat activist Aubrey Gordon describes healthism as the "key to pulling apart the ways in which size and health are used to write-off people who don't or can't perform health." She describes physical fitness, thinness, and the full functionality of body and mind as socially determined moral imperatives.

Healthism, fatphobia, ableism. Optimization. We value those bodies that grow nearer to Tolentino's ideal person. None of us will be her, and yet we can all measure ourselves in our distance from her.

And with the advancement of modern medicine, diet pills, and surgeries, and the outsourcing of time-sucking domestic labor, in concert with the capitalist American myth that *anyone can do anything as long as they want it enough*, we are all "able" to be ideal.

And if we can all be ideal, well then, I guess that makes those of us that aren't an example of moral failure. In Gordon's depiction of our anti-fat world, fatness is a presumed character flaw—one which, for her, brings about daily encounters with random strangers who "kindly" offer health advice or else give unrelenting commentary about how deserving she is of a base level of respect. When she tells her friends, normally empathetic people, about her daily hostilities, many of them tell her that those people might actually mean well. It's the equivalent of defending a homophobe by stating they "they just want you to be safe." Bleh.

Fatphobia, among all other marginalizations, is so deeply embedded into our cultural conscious that we even developed an entire measurement system to demonize fat folks[26] so that everyone else can feel justified in their fear of fatness and their intolerance toward the people that embody it.[27]

That same fear, instilled and reinforced in me by truly every person I encountered, drove me, as a fourteen-year-old, to starve myself, albeit briefly. That fear returned to me the night I sat in the hospital, refusing to accept the inability to regulate my fitness. I had never been free of a fatphobic consciousness—and, most likely, neither have you. Because the fearmongering

---

26  The BMI is a "medical" indicator based on totally arbitrary numbers; see Michael Hobbes's article "Everything You Know about Obesity is Wrong."

27  The fear of being ostracized is deeply embedded in us, through overt and subliminal messaging. Our culture's fatphobia entered into my psyche so seamlessly, I hardly understood it until I was made wiser by the important work of fat activists, many of whom have also paved the way for my political liberation as a queer person. I owe these folks, such as Aubrey Gordon, Lindy West, and my brilliant activist friend, Anna Burns, for their bravery—not for occupying the bodies that they do, but for actively speaking against a system that devalues fat folks.

   I cannot pretend that this essay does not center my life as a straight-sized person, which therefore distracts from the more important work being done by fat activists. I do hope that I can tie a thread between fatphobia and body dysmorphia that strengthens an argument against our social demand for perfection and thinness, one that straight-sized folks desperately need to understand so they can stop demonizing fatness.

masquerades as one of the most profitable industries in this country and adds to a series of emotional, celebratory weight loss narratives to boot.

That night in the emergency room, the doctors tried to put a cast on my leg. One of them put my foot to his shoulder like it was a rifle and bent my leg at a ninety-degree angle. They were trying to set the cast.

"Relax your leg," he said. He said it over and over again, and each time I thought I was as relaxed as I could be. His patience with me waned as he repeated himself and yet I found myself incapable of finding the rest he requested. He seemed unimpressed by my inability to take orders, but I had long been taking direction from a higher power. No one ever told me it was acceptable to relax.

"Letting yourself go" is an insult that speaks volumes, as if our natural and untamed selves would be monstrous threats to the social order. Those alien forms come lurking, and we try to ostracize ourselves from ourselves.

In my first days in bed, a girl I loved, but could never have, came to visit and I remarked upon my sprawling eyebrows; she touched my face to evaluate, and her hand traced a labyrinth on my forehead, following the path of my natural hair growth.

But she wasn't touching my eyebrows, she was touching me, and it felt good.

That summer, I practiced letting myself go. In bed, I caught myself clenching and would relax the muscles, allowing my body to sink an inch or more without my stalwart ass standing at full attention.

## The World Stopped

The girl who touched my eyebrows lent me her copy of Rilke's *Letters to a Young Poet* without realizing what poetry would do to my little gay heart. Rilke writes:

> *sickness is the means by which an organism frees itself from what is alien; so one must simply help it to be sick, to have its whole sickness and to break out with it, since that is the way it gets better ... you must be patient like someone who is sick, and confident like someone who is recovering.*

For years, I had been digging through myself. My nails have pinched pimples so incisively that the two crescent-shaped dents nearly met in the middle; I have gripped my love handles so hard that I almost convinced myself they were shrinking, always hoping to free myself from a personal inventory of my worst qualities—what I believed to be alien.

I believed that my sickness was my supply of stray hairs, or my haunches, or my stretchmarks, and that these were keeping me from fulfillment. But the sickness was the voice in my head that believed there was a boundary between my self and my body—that my self was only worthy of love if my body was without flaws. That is, without distinction from other, ideal, ordinary people. If I never felt beautiful, I at least felt valuable because of the discipline I was willing to enact on my body. I was optimizing, and I felt optimized. Exercise had been a form of disciplining my body. When I forced myself to run because I should, each step represented the sizing up of myself against someone else. I saw how I fell short, noticing how my body fell out of step with some perfectly timed beat, rather than acknowledging that I was a being that came from a place and a time.

Learning how to walk again brought me humility. It was a slow, painstaking process that involved the constant repetition of bodily mechanics: lift your heel twenty times and take a well-deserved break. I experienced gratitude—that my body could do anything at all.

I learned how to walk by understanding the thousands of tiny movements that make up a step. I saw my very panting as a form of beauty—that we can breathe is a miracle. For the very first time in my life, I smiled while running

I thought that I would never again take my body for granted. Whether it was walking, running, smiling, or writing, I thought I had learned to love my soul.

But I was still appreciating it for what it could *do* and for what it could prove. I walked to work, I walked home, I exercised, I ate healthy. I told people I was grateful to be able to run. I stayed trim. And that's the *thing*. The control that we're used to having over our own bodies—that's privilege. So I was proud of myself for this so-called wisdom—that sometimes our bodies need rest, not discipline. And that in itself is a trap of optimization: we rest so we can resume.

But then this body, and many others, went through the collective trauma of living during the time of COVID. Of course, there is so much to say about how COVID created two pandemics—one for the protected and one for those who had to sacrifice their safety for the ongoing business operations of this country. But in the very least, people knew a shared weariness. How unbelievably pathetic is it that more than six million people have lost their lives and the only thing we can agree upon is the fact that we're all exhausted?

While many folks had to deal with devastating health complications, stringent bosses delivering life-threatening ultimatums, an increasing number of hate crimes, and horrific losses of life, wealthy, white Americans grappled with a perceived loss of control.

Just like everyone else, I've had my unique quarantine epiphany. When everything in the world stopped, I stopped too. I started lounging, I started drinking more, I started smoking the occasional joint. I saw how much my body just wanted to find a way to relax.

And, like many others, I gained some quarantine weight. And many (many many many) people agreed that it was okay to go gray, to stop shaving, and to gain weight. But it is in the very act of consoling ourselves that we reveal our true feelings. Behind every Instagram post saying, "It's okay to feed your body because it's getting you through a crisis," is a blaring conditionality. The ideals of thinness, of productivity, of optimization, still exist, you just might catch a break every once in a while, like when you spend three months in a cast, or you spend eighteen months inside.

I don't think this nation has learned much at all about its attachment to an idealized version of personhood—to productivity, to beauty, to thinness—and I'm saying that as someone who keeps thinking they've learned their lesson about inner peace.

The best I can say is that I don't know much, except that it's hard to live in a world that deals in ideals. And every time we bring them up, we weaponize a fear of failure against anything foreign. As Rilke would remind us, that illness still remains. And after almost two years of an unfamiliar social order due to an ever-evolving virus, we're still waiting for our lives to go back to normal without wondering if that's really been working for us.

I don't have a solution, but, as with most things, I think we can all do better to question the assumptions we hold about good and bad, guilty and innocent, and simply try to share and listen in earnest. To loosen our grips on the control we think we might have over our lives, and the lives of those around us.[28]

---

28  In the almost five years that I've been thinking about and working on this essay, I have never found a good enough way to acknowledge my own privileges throughout my learning moments. At best, I glaze over the privilege of being able-bodied, straight-sized, and white. I can only tell my own story, but I can also use my story to advocate continued learning.

Three books that have had the greatest impact on my understanding of my privileged body, and how I have or have not recognized that privilege, have been Shrill by Lindy West, Exile and Pride by Eli Clare, and What We Don't Talk About When We Talk About Fat by Aubrey Gordon.

**Anniegram**

 **Annie Krabbenschmidt**
@krabbypatty415

# Still ...
# Coming Out

   Coming Out Day 2018

HAPPY COMING OUT DAY. It's not always glitter walls and double fisting, but it's so much better than being a version of myself that isn't authentic. Six years later, I can say coming out has brought me some of life's greatest gifts—friends, podcasts, recognition in the reputable Blotter magazine, girlfriends, heartbreaks, best friends, rhetorical tools in political arguments. I could go on and on. Because what I'm really saying is that coming out gave me my humanity, all wonderful, complicated, beautiful, and difficult aspects of it.

# Lovers & Friends*

*\* An actual ringtone I had on my Samsung flip camera phone when my "boyfriend" didn't invite me to his Six Flags birthday party.*

WHEN I LIVED in New York, one of my favorite activities was to take myself to the movies—a flaccid attempt to think of myself as, in the words of the great goddess Emma Watson, self-partnered. On a particular night in June, I had taken myself to a luxury theater in Chelsea to distract myself from yet another case of depression caused by unrequited love (self-partnering was obviously going swimmingly). I had long awaited the release of *Booksmart*—the 2019 (flawless, perfect) directorial debut of one Olivia Wilde.

If there is anything to be considered "nice" about having depression, it's that small things can make you think you've seen

Jesus herself. This was true about watching the *Booksmart* trailer. And it was true when I got to the theater: I was so excited to find out that the seats reclined that I looked up, pointed to a god I don't believe in, and whispered to myself, "Thanks, big guy."

The Cinélux in Chelsea has a floor plan with many cozy love seats. In another biblical miracle, my love seat was, for some reason, set apart from the rest of the cozy couches. I was an island.

This came in handy when, at movie's end, I found myself blubbering.

For me, and anyone with half a mind, this movie viewing experience was one of those where you're so aware that you're watching something stunning that you shouldn't even *try* to resist letting your jaw drop to the floor.

The high school comedy centers on two best friends, Molly and Amy—a valedictorian and a lesbian, respectively. It is friendship forward, with legs in fourth-wave feminism and tannins of raunchiness. It is, in the very core of its concept, committed to breaking the stereotypical depiction of girlhood.[29]

And then, in the final scene, as our two heroines part ways, a Lykke Li cover of "Unchained Melody," far more devastating than the original, plays over close-up shots of their faces while they fully absorb for the first time that they will be without each other for an entire year. In other words, nothing will ever be the same and change is the only constant. In OTHER other words, life has arrived for these two women.

---

[29] Tries to hold it in but can't help but scream, "IT'S THE BEST MOVIE OF ALL TIME!" before clasping hands over mouth.

That's when I started sobbing. And then I sat and sobbed through the entire credit sequence, during which the cast takes water-filled condoms to the face. And I continued sitting and sobbing in my singles' chair as the theater emptied.

I had walked into the movie feeling lonely, and I left feeling something slightly adjacent; in a rush, I was transported to the moment when my best friend, Maddie, had left for college the summer before my senior year of high school.

My *first* best friend came easily. After one shy encounter at the Panda Room, a kids' hair salon in Marin County, Jean and I learned that we were about to start kindergarten together. Around the second or third day of school, she asked if I wanted to be best friends and I accepted. We remained close, inseparable even, for my entire childhood.

I spent the first years of our friendship copying her every move. There were few ramifications for taking every Halloween costume idea she had, but I became aware that my lack of originality was a problem after one particular haircut, when I demanded that my hair be chopped to the same length as Jean's, just below her/my/our ears. I had not accounted for the fact that her hair was stick straight (and shiny and nice) and mine was Shirley Temple curly. I had walked into the salon with extreme confidence as I told the stylist what I wanted, and I left with hair that had sprung up into some ringleted mop.[30]

---

30 It's rumored that when the Jonas Brothers started their careers, they stole their look from that haircut of mine.

Like most youths, my sense of self was constantly fluctuating. I fixated on people and social identities as a way of feeling secure. While it is commonly ill-advised to find self-assurance in the external, before I was ready to accept that I was a lesbian repressing her sexuality, I took comfort in identifying myself by the company I kept.

In high school, I tried on a lot of versions of myself. Early on, I tried to be popular. There were more hair mistakes, like the side bangs I cut myself, which ended up looking like a mustache sitting atop my forehead. There were clear style faux pas, either because I wore what *I* wanted (jeans and my soccer sweatshirt) or because I wore what my mom, who shopped for me in her image at J.Crew, wanted. But then there was the fact that I was insecure and uncertain about the inkling in my gut that said, "There's just something a little off about that Krabbenschmidt girl."

As much as I could, I used humor—and an occasional stick of gum—as a way to charm people and make myself feel secure in my social world. I'm aware that this is not dissimilar to the way in which many charismatic authoritarian dictators are born: just a small person, with distressing hair and a J.Crew polo, orchestrating a social coup.

Despite the cardigans she "encouraged" me to wear, I probably do have my mother to thank for my ascent in the ranks of social power. At five foot two, she captained a Cadillac Escalade (oh yes, she did) and would drive members of my junior varsity basketball team across the Bay Area and provide snacks to boot. I didn't play more than three minutes that season, but on game days, I would be just as nervous as anyone, as I screamed into the phone, "Yes, that's *three* turkey sandwiches and *one* roast beef!"

I handpicked who would be in my carpool every day. I would point my finger with the ease of a reclining woman in a renaissance painting, selecting the chosen few. Oh, I was simply drunk with the power.

And in my ascent, I felt that my life was basically successful. It *seemed* like self-actualization when I eventually made my way to the inner circles of the upper strata.

But I was faking my belonging—always feeling inauthentic and stuck and, often, disgusted with myself. It never occurred to me that my sister and I might need different things in our high school experiences. I was so possessed by the drive to be popular that I stole my parents' liquor, hosted parties I really hated, and smoked hand-rolled joints made from particularly dry pages of the bible. I would do it all, if only to get attention (and, dare I say, love?) from cool girls in my class.

When my friends started having sex, I knew my contortions wouldn't make their way to a bedroom any time soon. I simply could not fake a desire to be with men. Did I crave intimacy? Well, I started to cry every time I was drunk or high in the hope that one particular girl, Hailey, would turn her head from a collection of boys who fawned over her to comfort me, so I'd say yeah, I craved intimacy. As an adult, I still catch the occasional whiff of Aquolina Pink Sugar perfume, which smells like a sexy mix between crème brûlée and a vanilla Yankee Candle, and feel a confusing tingle in my tummy.

Oh yes, that tingle is a reminder of how desperately I longed for the girls I loved to love me back.

In my head, best friendship was a form of undying loyalty. A best friend was someone who would rather spend time cuddling me than being with boys, I thought, because I didn't have a word for my sexuality.

On one cool Bay Area night, Hailey left me with the two German exchange students she was hosting that summer so that she could go into the woods to smoke weed with boys. My new friends taught me to say "Kiffen ist nicht gut, Miststück!" which roughly translated to mean, "Smoking weed is bad, bitch!" Hell hath no fury like a woman scorned. Given that I, too, smoked weed to impress peers, I had the nagging feeling in my chest that this was less about the weed and more about the boys that supplied it to Hailey.

These slights would occur, and I felt so painfully alone. I was disappointed in friends who didn't text me as often as I wanted them to and frustrated with myself for wanting too much.

I sought best friends the way other people seek romantic partners. My desperate hope was that finding one, *the one*, might offer a sense of grounding. Of course, due to our previous conclusion that I was being inauthentic *and* that nothing external can save us, that grounding never came. Instead, I often found myself with an empty chest—a feeling I now know to call heartbreak.

After more than two years in a constant cycle of searching, finding, and losing, I started hanging out with an altogether different group of folks. These incredible people in the grade above me were neither popular nor unpopular. They existed as a unit that cared deeply for each other in a way I hadn't seen among high schoolers. Their coed friend group was fiercely loyal to one another, and the boys looked after the girls like sisters, and no one thought to kiss one another, which was, shockingly enough, the exact environment I thrived in.

The two girls in this group were my friends from the soccer team; one of them was this uber cool, uber smart athlete/genius who intimidated the hell out of me and the other was Maddie.

It's hard to identify when Maddie and I became best friends. It could have been the time when I applied for the a cappella group she was in and she couldn't stop laughing throughout my very sincere audition, or the first time we drove together, belting songs at the top of our lungs (agreeing not to discuss my audition), or the time she called me on a Friday night because she'd had an allergic reaction to an orange and all her other friends were at a party but she knew I would be free.

But perhaps what brought us together most coherently was our tendency to opt out of typical high school sexual encounters. On the same night in the early spring of my junior year, the two of us made out with the boys that would eventually be our prom dates. A few weeks later, as our commitments to these boys were made, we each validated the other's sudden desire to skip the night altogether. And when we ditched the after-prom party, and our dates, so I could go to her house and fall asleep spooning her, I felt that my behavior was perfectly normal, since my best friend had said it was. In that sense, Maddie was the first person who made me feel not so freakish.

That spring and summer, I did my very best to immerse myself in her life. In addition to spooning her every night that I could, I also woke up early to make her the tea that she liked. I learned all the lyrics to *The Eminem Show* so that we could rap them in her car together. I went to dinner parties, and family gatherings, and broke one of the cardinal rules of being a Krabbenschmidt, which is that we avoid public water parks at all costs. Yet there I was, one hot July day, sitting in a shallow pool of water mixed with sweat, sunscreen, and possibly urine, as we waited in line for a multistory tubular ride.

When her family moved out of their model home and into the identical home next door, I was among the many who accidentally carried things from the new house back into the old one because that is how similar they were. And I was happy. And I felt loved.

And then one morning in mid-August, we woke up at the crack of dawn (well, *I* woke up at the crack of dawn and then woke Maddie up with tea moments later) so she could move to Los Angeles for college. I shed a single tear.

There is something extra vulnerable about trying to stop yourself from crying; you show not just the emotion, but also the  failing effort to hide it. And, of course, Maddie wasn't crying at all, because why would she? It wasn't her heart ripping out of its chest as her black Toyota Camry turned the corner, off to a new beginning.

When she was out of sight, I went back up to the room I had helped her move into and cried into her purple sheets. That's the memory that suddenly flooded my mind as *Booksmart* ended.

It never would have occurred to me then that I was a lesbian. But more accurately, it occurred to me every single day of my young life. Our brains, however, are sneaky little eels that can find a way to sell us on anything. I was quite good at rationalizing my way out of my gay suspicions and into an assured straightness. Justifications included, "I just like spending time with her," "Everyone has close friendships," "Cuddling releases oxytocin into the brain!" and "I'm not in love, I'm just obsessed!"[31]

In what was perhaps my first foray into an eventual lifetime of dealing with anxiety, I let my mind whirr with adequate demonstrations of my heterosexuality until I felt comforted by the honest-to-god truth—that I was a salt-of-the-earth "straight lady" looking forward to my "first time" with someone "really special."

I could still find a way to fit within the bounds of what was expected of me as a woman. Of course, this involved obeying quite a few rules. The rules were sometimes domestic, sometimes social, sometimes spoken, sometimes unspoken. Most importantly, their blended concoction was some elixir that promised to secure desirability, acceptability, and unbounded success.

There are certain people who serve as deified vehicles through which the sacred rules of the social order come to life.

---

[31] Which was, somehow, considered more acceptable?

## Fred

There's Emily Post, Dr. Spock, and my mother. She taught me everything I know about cocktail napkins and table settings. I can identify the subtle differences between tasteful and tacky. I know the mark of a good wine and a bad, bad houseguest.

A bad houseguest wears a backwards baseball hat and sweatpants, and has a messy room, and laughs either too loudly or too quietly; a good house guest doesn't let depression, or even teenage angst, get in the way of a carefully planned dinner party. I lived for my first eighteen years of life as a bad, not good, house guest.

For a long while, approval captivated me, and I did try to hold parts of myself back.

But I *wants* to wear sweatpants, precious.

The great irony of Homo sapiens is that we are a *chaos* of genetic variations, and all we *are* is a bundle of quirks and imperfections. Yet, it seems that the mission of the social species to bury these things deep, deep down—it's "rude" to take up space with quirks and imperfections.

My weirdness, my burping, my sensitivity, my emotional life, my depression—I dared myself to live the rest of my life without burdening people with these truths about me. Which worked for a while and then unraveled—slow at first, and then fast, fast, fast.

Even though Maddie made me feel safer than anyone I had ever met, I was no closer to exposing myself as flawed at sixteen. In all my years of childhood, I never once called a friend crying. Not over boys, not over girls, and not over my feelings about either. About once a month, I allowed myself to cry while bathing, but even then, it was because I could hardly distinguish my sobs from the sound of water sputtering from an old shower head.

When I came out to Robin, and subsequently everyone else, and then started dating Paige, my life felt so different than it had been at seventeen. The good was that I had discovered love, blah blah blah, everyone in my family and circle of friends had accepted my sexuality with the kindest open arms, blah blah blah, I was able to live more authentically, blah blah blah[32]. The bad was that I lost touch with almost everyone from high school. I assumed that the more I leaned into my queerness, the more I would have to distance myself from any of my former selves. Maddie would, quite tragically, have to be cut from my life too. Even as I braved starting a new, gay life, it felt scary to change right before someone's eyes as I tried (and sometimes failed) to make things fit. That's ... vulnerable.

When Maddie and I reconnected one awkward summer night, years after graduating, I felt alienated from her. The fact that she brought her roommate, Wolfee, only made me feel more distant. We had lost touch for a few years. I had visited her at school and occasionally saw her on breaks, but we seemed to be growing into two different lives.

And yet, it turned out that I was wrong about that.

Call it a form of supernatural intelligence, but when Wolfee picked a small piece of chicken tikka masala out of Maddie's

---

[32] It's almost like it would take me an entire book to explain how much subtext is in the blah blah blah.

teeth, suddenly the puzzle—the giant kind that toddlers use to learn general motor skills—came clearly into focus. Maddie and Wolfee were not just roommates, they were also best friends.

Obviously, I'm joking. The fact that the two of them were clearly in a queer partnership finally explained why Maddie had avoided her prom date to spoon with me.

Later in the evening, we went to a concert, and when Wolfee stepped to a back corner of the room, I told Maddie what she would no doubt have already learned from one of our mutual friends: that I was gay.

After a silence that was heavy with inevitability, Maddie confessed that she, too, was gay.

"Yeah. I know," I said triumphantly, "You're dating Wolfee." My self-righteousness would allow us both to avoid a more intimate conversation. Perhaps I had grown softer after falling in love, but I wasn't really ready to talk openly about the nuances of being queer. All my friends at Duke accepted the fact that I was gay and didn't ask questions, and that was fine with me. Maddie and I avoided talking about our feelings for a good long time.

Then Paige broke up with me. And it was like every fear or sadness I'd ever had needed tending to. I was living at my parents' house when it happened, and by coincidence, Maddie was in the Bay Area that same weekend. In an act of generosity that was not precedented by any efforts on my part to be a good friend in the preceding fourteen months, Maddie was at my house within forty-eight hours of my breakup. She found me tucked into the corner of an L-shaped sectional with a steady stream of tears falling down my shell-shocked face. I couldn't imagine a more shameful state for someone to see me in and assumed that it was moments like this that probably made me unworthy of Paige's love in the first place.

I was lost in just about every possible way after the breakup. That relationship was one of the only things that had sustained me in my last two years at Duke. It was a very nice distraction from an underpinning lack of security in my sense of self.

Throughout our relationship, I had let Paige's needs override finding myself, and I was happy to do so, because who actually wants to stare into the dark abyss of the soul and meet whatever demons are waiting there? I learned that fighting was bad, and crying was bad, and complaining about her ignoring me when she was out with her lacrosse team was also bad. So I was feeling lonely and feeling bad about being lonely.

Career-wise, I may never know what's going on. At the time of writing this sentence, I have absolutely no idea if this book is going to be published or if it will sit in a computer file. But in terms of knowing myself and knowing my worth—I committed to that undertaking in the wake of heartbreak. And Maddie—and also Leah, and Robin, and Katelin, among others—helped me do that.

When I say "others," I do want to make it clear that I'm including the honorable Julie B., my therapist.

After visiting New York, I told Julie how scared I had been to be approached by women at Cubbyhole.

"Annie," she started, "is it okay to like girls?"

"Yes," I replied half-heartedly before I started crying. She wasn't asking if it was okay to *be* a gay person. She was asking if it was okay for me, Annie, to be attracted to women.

"Don't you think you were in love with a lot of people as a kid?" she asked (Cristine's name on a cubby, a letter I wrote to yet another friend, Meghan, when I was eight telling her how much I had missed her over the weekend, Aquolina Pink Sugar spritz). "Weren't you in love with Maddie?"

I was speechless.

"But I couldn't have been in love with Maddie," I offered. "We had sleepovers, Julie. We *spooned*." Didn't that make me threatening in my attraction?

Then Julie told me the story of an adolescent relationship in which two people cared deeply for each other and took care of each other, and she told me it was mine. It wasn't something gross. It was something absolutely beautiful.

And now that I've been dumped so many times that it's almost comical (I said almost), I can confirm that all relationships are intangible nebulae of their own unique kinds. You simply cannot know how many types of love there are out there.

There's Maddie, who was the first queer(ish) partner(ish) I ever had. She made me feel funny, and loveable, and, yes, special; Robin, who took me under her wing and forced me to face my fears; Leah and Katelin who both experienced me at my best, but also lived with me through my absolute worst;[33] There's my best friend Claire, whom I've known since the day she was born—two months after I was—and whose house is the only one I feel

---

[33] Leah would have me tell you that when I broke my leg, she truly nursed me back to health. A certified non-toucher, like myself, Leah helped me wash my hair in the kitchen sink, while I cried about how incapable I felt (a reminder of how privileged my life as an able-bodied person has been); I'm pretty sure it was the worst day of her life, but the fact that she did it to help me. That's what it means to find unconditional love.

comfortable entering uninvited; and there's Paige, who taught me what it meant to feel desired—and taught me that there was more to a healthy relationship than that.

Queer folks often have unconventional relationships, but this makes all the more sense when you think about the fact that we often don't share the same cultural roots as our own two parents. We need all the love we can get—the love of parents, the love of friends, the love of the community, or, sometimes, the love of a best friend that resembles a romance but is really just the deepest form of care. And I guess what I'm saying is that I deserve to feel loved and supported, and I deserve to love myself enough to require that in any relationship.

This lesson, which I am still actively learning, was hard to accept at first. But as I ventured further into the chaos of my twenties, I started to acknowledge that even if I had a hard time asking for it, I *needed* support.

So, I started calling friends. I called with snot dripping from my nose, I called with panic attacks about work projects, and I called just so that they could tell me that they loved me. At first, these calls scared me, and I would apologize over and over again for calling; and while what I said was "I'm sorry to call you like this," what I meant was "I'm sorry to *be* like this." As they patiently talked me off whatever ledge I was on, I was beginning to process that real love is unconditional.[34]

Julie pointed out to me that the strength of my friendship with Maddie may have started as a romantic relationship for me at seventeen, but it ended up being my first, true "found family" moment. A good family member doesn't love you when it's con-

---

34  See previous footnote.

venient—they love you even when they are annoyed beyond belief with you. It's familial love like this—whether it's between you and your immediate blood relatives or you and your gay best friend—that holds you together when you want to fall apart.

Despite my conviction that I would never love again after Paige, it wasn't long after moving to New York that I met Stephanie. It was my first relationship as an out queer person, and it was quick and fierce. But, man, is it fun to fall in love. To think all day about a person who's got you head over heels. To brag to your friends about that person's green eyes, or freckled nose, or funny hand gestures. And I was so unbelievably in love with sweet Stephanie.

She made me feel loved, too. Attractive even. She told me everything I had always desperately, secretly, wanted to hear: that I was special, one of a kind, and that she wanted to spend all her time by my side. As with every relationship, I overcame certain fears. I wore a suit for the first time, and Stephanie thought I looked—and this is her word, not mine—"hot." Hot!!! Oh, how I blush.

So then Stephanie dumped me suddenly, and while that could have caused all sorts of trust issues within me, instead it taught me that heartbreak feels better when you've put your entire heart on the line. The risk is worth it to know a person's love like that and to have them know yours.

When I fell in love again—despite proclaiming that after Stephanie, I could never love another soul—it was slower and a little more careful. Katie was a close friend of mine. I waited until I was sure she was the kind of person I could call crying. When I reached that point of certainty, when she had said enough times that she'd never had a friend like me and that she felt uniquely seen and supported in our friendship, there was nothing left to do but confront my feelings and share them.

I had dated, I had loved, I had crushed, but this would be the first time in my life that I would take a big, bold swing for love. My biggest fear loomed before me: the fear of burdening people with my feelings, my sexuality, and my desires, and the rejection that might follow. But having my found family in my corner—knowing that there was someone out there who had loved me through the deepest of my feelings and the foreignness of my sexuality—made me sure that radical honesty was the only way to find out who loves you in this world.

Not Katie, as it turned out. The rejection stung a lot more than Stephanie's had, and it came with a very lengthy period of self-loathing and wondering what step I had missed in my journey to get Katie to fall in love with me.

And that was the issue. With Katie, with Stephanie, with Paige, I had bent over backwards to win their favor. Some instances were more harmless than others. Making tea for Maddie was no big deal, but letting Katie use me for two a.m. affirmations, letting her call when she needed me and disappear when she didn't—that's a form of self-harm. As Julie told me, I was in it for the torture.

"Well, then," I asked, "what do I have to do to get someone who would fight for me?"

And even as the words left my mouth, I realized that I had an entire army of people trying to fight for me—who had lifted me up when I wanted to sink. The only person, it would seem, who adamantly refused to fight for me, was, well, me.

I was the last person willing to stand up for myself. For two years after Katie, before leaving New York for Los Angeles, I practiced fighting for my needs the way a best friend would. Some people stuck around, and some people didn't.

I was realizing that I deserved love of a certain kind, regardless of whether a relationship was between friends, family, partners, friends that feel like family, friends that feel like partners.

Then, despite believing in my very core that Katie was the only person I had ever, could ever, would ever, truly love, Rian came along shortly after I moved to Los Angeles. She asked if we could kiss and hug without really being *together*. And as much as I wanted to say we could, and that I'd happily fulfill her needs instead of taking care of mine, I didn't.

And just because I'm a drama queen, I told her, while wearing my rainbow overalls and Birkenstocks, "I'm not your backburner girl," before walking away.

Are you kidding me? That is *so* good!

Ironically or not, Rian was the one who came walking after me. At the time of writing this, Rian is my best friend, my partner, and, it often seems, my family.

**Anniegram**

 **Annie Krabbenschmidt**
@krabbypatty415

# Oh, I Get it, You Never Stop Coming Out

  Coming Out Day 2020

For me, I have never not understood my coming out story with a mental health journey. I was totally shell-shocked by my realization that I was gay (no matter what my dad predicted!!). It hit me like a ton of bricks and then I sat with bricks in my belly for over a year, weighed down and stuck. Just stuck. I didn't want to date men (le ew), but coming out would mean dealing with a permanent inability to please the patriarchy. I would, forever more, be a disappointment.

I know, I know—I'm not a disappointment, I'm delightful, my hair looks better than anyone could have predicted. But the real truth is that we all live with expectations about what our futures are going to look like. Our families and friends have an idea of what we're going to grow into, whether they know it or not. Our culture has

**Anniegram**

an idea of what we're going to grow into (monogamous, married, settled down, Monday night football, idk whatever you straights do). And deviating is threatening. Especially when you make no promises about where you're headed next. You can't send postcards from a place called Limbo.

But with growth, and the repeated mantra that I'm going to be loved, that I am loved, I learned to have fun in the middle. Years after coming out, I'm still adjusting aspects of my presentation and my identity. I'm still playing with pronouns, playing with the notion of home and family. This year, on coming out day, I want to remind you about fluidity—yes, you too, straights! You can play with expectations, take a big risk, try something else. The spirit of Coming Out Day is to celebrate authenticity. Finding that is a hard journey for EVERYONE. I'm not recommending that you appropriate this holiday from vulnerable queers, but I'm suggesting that if we lived in a world with a little more bravery to be flexible, creative, and surprising—where hair is just a thing you can cut without consequence—with fewer boxes, then we could *all* be a little more liberated. And maybe breaking free from some of our patriarchy trappings, we can all enjoy ourselves enough to stop caring about who's f***ing whom and what a "real" family or marriage looks like.

# Apple Cider
# Donuts

If you get off Connecticut Route 190 and head north on Gunpowder Lane, past Giuseppe's Brook, past Pine Field Drive, past *Avery* Brook, past Chris's Squirrels and More, past Barn Swallow Drive, past the spook house, you will eventually come to a discreet driveway—the grand entrance, as was always my opinion, to the place I spent most of my summers and winters as a kid: Nonie and Pop's.

Coming up the winding gravel way was a drama of its own. You had to drive slow to avoid disturbing the gravel or grazing a tree, and you had to cross over yet another brook. It was basically the opening of a Jane Austen film adaptation—a stifled city girl takes a breath of fresh air. Except instead of spending my holiday riding sidesaddle behind a brooding, dark-haired bachelor, my ideal summer would have me riding a John Deere lawn mower, normal saddle.

## Fred

Every moment of the journey from the street to the front porch was full of wonder. I mentioned the brook, but did I mention the bright red gazing ball, lackadaisically sitting in a bed of ivy? My sister and I would sit with our noses pressed to the window of the car, trying to take everything in at once. On the front porch (a real porch, I tell you!) there was a single bench, which hung from a delicate chain. We'd spend our nights sitting there, keeping watch over summer storms as they rolled in, or fireflies, as they blinked off in the distance. With enough citronella candles for a séance, we could sit for hours, believing that this rural world could do us no harm.

This was a world primed for adventure, a manifest destiny for urban dwellers like my sister and me. In the winters, this meant building an igloo or a snowman; in the summers, this meant insect-gathering expeditions across the brook. Though the brook was only about two hundred feet from the porch, I packed my canteen with water and double-checked my survivor's toolbelt all the same. A walking stick would be needed as well, there was no question about it. We were prepared for the elements. Even my older sister, normally so neatly put together, wouldn't mind catching a critter—with a net, at least.

It was a place that represented total freedom to me. I could play with anything, from dirt to Pop's fishing rods. Every day, we'd pile into his hunter-green pickup truck and get wrapped up in something magnificent. Sometimes, we'd find ourselves at Coconut's Lounge, discreetly scratching off lottery tickets under the table. Other times, we'd drive around, and Pop would detail every haunting the town had ever had.

No man better epitomized the town of Somers, Connecticut than he did. A real man's man, he bought me my first Swiss Army pocketknife and spent the afternoon in his garage etching my initials into it. He could pass hours out at his bench, smoking pipe tobacco, making all sorts of things with nothing but his tools. When he made four matching coatracks—their heights corresponding to those of my older sister, my two younger cousins, and me—I believed I'd never again know such luxury. A coat rack!

My summer educational program consisted of accompanying my grandfather as he ran errands that seemed exotic to me, like going to the dump. With our favorite Patsy Cline tape in the deck, the two of us would warble about our heartache and our man's cheating heart, getting nearly drunk on our bottles of sarsaparilla soda.

During one of my many summer breaks spent there, I stared wistfully at cattle farms and cornfields and told my mother that I wanted to live in a town just like Somers when I was older. She kept her lips tight. Not even a mother's intuition could have prepared her to appreciate the irony in my statement: that I would eventually come out as gay and become the family's lone radical feminist, a flag bearer for political correctness, was fundamentally at odds with the declaration that Somers was the greatest place on earth.

· X · X · X ·

## Fred

Somers is a small New England town with a cultural identity that more closely resembles a Southern one. Thanks to the local tobacco business, Somers was, and is, a farmland. People own modestly sized houses on big properties. But even the richest resident of Somers mows his own lawn every Saturday morning. Above all else, Somers residents are defiantly conservative in their values—hard work among the most important of them—and in their politics.

My mom grew up in this tiny town, in a time when women took home economics and men took shop. She had a big personality—so big as to be somewhat indecent. She was like an artist without a medium, unable to help the fact that her charisma made her the center of attention.

Though she couldn't sing a note on key, she harbored a deep resentment when she wasn't chosen for the school's Christmas choir, heartbroken that she wouldn't have her opportunity to shine in front of her classmates. She received multiple detentions for disturbing classes, just by asking the wrong questions or making ill-timed jokes. On some occasions, it was nothing more than the way she carried herself. She was nearly suspended when she addressed a teacher by her first name, Judy.

"Jud-day. Jud-ay, Jud-ay," she exclaimed with accompanying finger guns. Whether her punishment was because she violated a more literal code of conduct by using a teacher's first name or because her outburst had too much rhythm is anyone's guess.

She never saw a future for herself in Somers. Her parents crushed her desire to go to culinary school because it was for men. And after graduating college, her life was an unending cycle of going from her job as a Friendly's sundae specialist to her job as a waitress and then back home to her childhood bedroom, where she would cry into her red shag carpet about a college boyfriend who had cheated on her. This would continue until eventually she would marry, move out of her parents' home, and into her husband's.

Somewhere around the age of twenty-two or twenty-three, she packed up and left with no intention of returning. This was not a town that people left, and everyone waited, perhaps with too much spite, for her to return. Their prediction was that she'd be back within six months. She borrowed $600 from her cousin and flew to California without a job or a place to live.

San Francisco would have been the perfect fantasy world—one where she walked crisp city streets in oversized sunglasses, and where no one would bat an eye at someone feeling eccentric enough to wear a beret and ascot.

My mom must have looked at the Golden Gate Bridge and seen a gateway to her very destiny. I saw it and thought a little bit about death. That's not so surprising, considering the iconography of the landmark, but as a teenager, I wondered how much thinking about it was too much. It's not that I was necessarily suicidal, but I was pretty sure that few of my classmates had to reassure themselves that they weren't.

I went from a grimacing adolescent to a grimacing teenager. I sulked, I despaired, I briefly starved myself. I would experience bouts of inescapable discomfort with my life. Playing soccer was almost the only thing that brought me any joy. I wasn't a strong player, and yet I felt that there was nothing else I was meant to do in this universe.

Soccer season meant grass stains, mud, shorts, and a team-wide loyalty to men's deodorant—even from the pretty girls. And that made me feel at home. I would leave for school in the morning with a bag packed to last me until 7:00 or 8:00 at night. My mom stopped expecting me for dinner altogether. I was just a specter in the house that would trail filthy soccer socks down the hallways.

Given my secret life as a member of the cult of Old Spice, I was all the more resentful when I was expected to appear at family social events—well-shaven and wearing a dress. It was a cruelty I fought with disdain for both my parents and their friends.

In the unspoken rules of a civilized society, there seemed to be a code I couldn't crack. After my first week of college, I realized that at least part of my misunderstanding had to do with the fact that I was, and had been all this time, gay. Things clicked into place. My sulking, my misery, my inability to understand my mother's wardrobe requirements—all were mostly explained by my repressed queerness.

I realized that maybe I'd had a hard time connecting with the people who had brought me up because I would have rather actively rejected them than explain myself—which, for many years, I couldn't have done. Then I fell in love. While I had always thought of myself as emotionally blunt, snide, sarcastic, and frankly, mean, falling in love made me permanently soft.

The fall of my junior year at Duke, I was falling in love with my secret girlfriend, and Pop was falling ill. He hadn't really been well for years. When I was fourteen, he'd had a stroke, which caused a car accident, and he hadn't been the same since. As a man who had always loved to take to his couch after a long day, he slowly became both couch-ridden and couch-like, sagging in his cheeks, his ears, his lower eyelids. He was barely recognizable to us—and we to him. When we visited, he would ask us if we had ever been to his house before, as if we hadn't come of age there. If we said that we hadn't been there, we would ask him to give us a tour of the house. He would then decide that we had in fact been to the house before and didn't need a tour. The line separating physical ability from depression was never really clear to us.

My mother called me one morning while I was catching up on assignments that had been abandoned in order to spend my evening with Paige. She was boarding a flight to Connecticut to visit Pop in the hospital. She wanted to know whether I would like to meet her in Connecticut. She'd always wanted me to see New England in the fall.

I was a little conflicted. On the one hand, Paige was at away games for the weekend, and I would have to find some way to spend my weekend to distract myself from wondering if she missed me as much as I missed her. On the other, I had a big secret I was hiding from my family. Living a clear double life creates distance between your two worlds.

But I was love-struck. Sometimes, it felt like I wanted to hold *everyone's* hand. And I was starting to figure out an explanation for what seemed like fundamental differences between me and the people that raised me—one in particular, that I thought I might one day want to share with them.

It was jarring to drive up that front way one gloomy fall afternoon, full of dread instead of excitement. Pop wasn't inside grilling hot dogs and frying potatoes. He was at a hospital down the road. My favorite aunt advised me not to see Pop in the hospital because he didn't recognize anyone and said nasty things to people helping him. There was always a risk that seeing him in such a way might replace my good memories with him, but it had been years since I'd had any. I decided to see him.

My mom and I went to the hospital together, and she prepped me for disappointment. But the moment I walked in the room, he looked straight at me and smiled. With full recognition, he asked, "What are you doing here?" I wasn't expecting that. How do you bury someone who suddenly comes to life?

I told him—or tried to, through tears—that I was there to bust him out. "My motorcycle is parked out front, and I'm going to get you out of here in a sidecar," I lied. He was a man who loved tall tales, and it seemed to be the only fitting explanation that I could give him. Even as I wanted to believe it myself, the room returned to its reality. In his hospital bed, Pop looked deflated. It appeared as if someone had just scooped half of him away, a couch without cushions.

He was thirsty and asking, begging, his nurse to give him water. He was at risk for pneumonia, so she gave him a wet sponge to suck. While he kept begging for more, my mom told him that we had to get going. She didn't want me to see him debased and desperate. I hugged him and choked out my goodbye, knowing full well it was for the last time.

My mom and I walked arm in arm back to the car. We spent the weekend together in her New England town, doing things I always thought were myths of a time gone by—as it turns out, corn mazes are very much a thing.

We carted a wheelbarrow full of pumpkins around a farm. We stopped at an apple farm, which had its very own apple farm souvenir shop run out of a barn. We found one dozen apple cider donuts. And while we barreled through all twelve of them, I looked at her like there was no better delicacy in all the world, and she looked back at me like she'd always wanted to tell me so. We hiked a quarter mile to the top of Soapstone Mountain and looked out at a shallow valley below, which rolled much more gently than the dramatic topography of the California coast.

The trees below us were ablaze with fall color, every leaf suddenly defined in its singularity, thanks to reds and oranges that we Californians could only imagine. And I saw my mother as a child of *this* place. Stripped of her social duties, she was still a silly kid pointing finger guns, who looked an awful lot like, well, me, who was once kicked out of class for singing Nat King Cole's "L-O-V-E" in the middle of a lesson.

· X · X · X ·

My mom and I shared her childhood bedroom that weekend in Connecticut. I had my own twin bed in the room across the upstairs landing, but I don't think either of us wanted to be like Pop—lying in bed alone.

We leafed through her Somers High yearbook. There she was with her big hair and fake tan, looking charismatic and beloved, even in photographs.

Somewhere near the back of the book, a note was scrawled around a senior's headshot, which bore a strong resemblance to Dorothy from the Golden Girls. The note from Rita started, "Dawn, you dear thing, you."

"Oh Rita," my mom sighed. "She used to pick me up on her scooter. We would ride around town all night. We had a hoot."

And then, these words, which shook me to my very core:

"She left town pretty soon after graduating and came out of the closet. I think she's happier now down in Florida somewhere. Oh, I loved that big old lesbian."

Growing up in an affluent suburb of San Francisco, I had never met a lesbian, and I assumed that my mom hadn't either. At best, my town had a beloved gay hairdresser, Christopher, but everyone knows that's different. I've never owned a hair dryer in my life.

My mother was a socialite—world's most gracious host, timeless style, knows the exact purpose of each wine glass she owns. I was a tomboy—t-ball champion, tree climber, obsessed with construction. The conflict between us over my wardrobe, my etiquette, and my demeanor was like a constant, silent brooding. While our verbal sparring kept only a semi-regular schedule, there was just a core misalignment of our values that lurked under the surface of every interaction we had, all of which felt like veiled criticisms of my very being. The subtext was that she was just waiting for me to finally be the daughter she'd been shopping for her whole life.

My mother left a town that often told her that she couldn't and arrived in a city that allowed her to reply, "Watch me." Despite the scraping by—living in windowless garage apartments, working three jobs at once, eating ninety-nine cent boxed cornbread for almost every meal, crying from young adult existentialism—her life in San Francisco was painted in full color.

One of her first three jobs she took in exchange for clothes. She carried herself through the city, broke but well dressed. When my parents first started dating, my dad was shocked to learn that my mother didn't own a bed. Her glamorous exterior was her survival instinct on display, because her status was, and may always threaten to be, precarious. Close in her wake was the shadow of her origins—a farm town that didn't understand her, nor she it. Something, it would seem, that we have deeply in common.

I, too, sought to escape the version of womanhood laid out for me. I resented my parents' world, where a minimalist wardrobe was a sign of dereliction and a tattoo was a sign of absolute derangement.

My mother thrives on being pleasant and palatable. But she's more than that. On her bed, looking through a class of '78 yearbook, I briefly saw her as others do: a friend to all meek and mighty, open-minded, and unfailingly warm. Knowing that she rode on the back of Rita's scooter, presumably with her arms tightly wrapped around a lesbian, I knew that she was the kind of person who could parent her gay child.

My grandpa died, as grandparents do. At the funeral, I remember gazing upon his embalmed face. It alarmed me to see him with a caked-on layer of foundation and a set of rosy cheeks that was much more "performing at the cabaret" than "driving to the dump in winter." And it pained me to realize that I was inspecting him more closely than I ever had before. It's a cruel process of grief to sort through someone's remains to try and finally understand them once and for all. Somehow, we all forget to really *see* the people we love when they're alive and well.

A week after the funeral, I went home for Thanksgiving. On Wednesday, I came out to my family. Only my sister was surprised.

On Thursday, we went to a very typical Marin County dinner party. But for the first time, I felt like I was in cahoots with my family. We now shared an understanding among us that, frankly, is all we want when we look for community.

When we got home, my mom and I were in her bathroom. She flitted gruffly about until she just stopped and burst into tears. I scooped her up into my arms, like there was no gulf between us at all.

"I miss my dad," she cried. Her father hadn't really been himself for years, so missing him in that moment didn't make much sense, but death evades logic, and dead parents make daughters out of all of us.

In the years since that fall weekend, my mom and I have sometimes been distant, but mostly, we've been close. I made her cry when I shaved my head, but every time I visit my parents, I can't help but wake up early and bring three mugs of coffee for us to share in bed while they catch me up on town news. And my mom and I like to travel as a duo. When I graduated college, we went to cooking school in Ireland together. Two weeks sharing a tiny dorm room, and all we could do was roll around complaining that we had become bread loaves. We would sniff the garlic under our fingernails with an addict's compulsion.

"Oh my god, it's foul!" we'd say over and over in between hits.

We were like Lucy and Ethel, lighting fire to baked dishes and covering up dented pastries with strategic floral arrangements. Alone in a vacuum, the two of us could have had a very successful comedy act—as our fellow Irish classmates insisted. And when we were out of our usual contexts, just being people, covered in raw chicken, the two of us were a team.

Three years later, when I graduated from my master's program, we took our trip to Woodstock, Vermont, where she told me I shouldn't dress like such a clown. But when I finally moved to New York later that fall, where I'd spend the next two years really growing up, there was a package waiting for me in the mail room. In it was a velvet-lined box containing the pocket watch I had wanted from the vintage shop where I bought my first writer's blazer. With it was a note from my mom that read, "It's your time." A vote of confidence that she had my back.

Sometimes my mom has a hard time understanding me as more than just her daughter. She sees my heart and she sees my head, but she cannot understand my hairy legs. And somehow, for parents and children, it is those things that seem to stand out. Every so often, she even sees a dress she thinks I might like.

As I step out of my room in a button-down flannel instead, I see her look me up and down before deciding whether it's too late to instill crucial life lessons in me. She'll propose, from time to time, that I "could be the kind of lesbian who wears skirts, you know." There's no amount of explanation that I could give that would convince her that skirts go against every aspect of my being, lesbian or not.

Some connections need a time machine—or at least a moped scooter. Because if I were my mother's classmate, I would probably have called her dear thing. Thirty years earlier, she might have even been my best friend. Our only real problem is that I am her daughter, and she is my mother. And we are, to this day, two people who dared to dream of an elsewhere far from home.

**Anniegram**

 **Annie Krabbenschmidt**
@krabbypatty415

# Okay, I'm Done Here

   **Coming Out Day 2021**

I'm honestly too busy thriving in my life, chasing my wildest dreams as an author, and feeling freer than I've ever felt, as a genderqueer literal icon, to post for #nationalcomingoutday and THAT'S a perfect #nationalcomingoutday post

# Introvert's Burlesque

I HAD JUST DECIDED to move to New York when my therapist, Julie, gave me a shocking piece of news. After about a year of meeting together, we were on a schedule wherein I would have my mind blown by buried feelings that were lingering as traumas once a week. It all started when she asked me to identify a feeling in the pit of my stomach, which was shame, and I responded by tearfully regurgitating long-forgotten memories of being scolded.

On this particular day, Julie gave me the news that I was an introvert.

Being of the atheistic generation that clings desperately to the guidance of Myers–Briggs personality types—and of course, the stars—I was identifying at the time as an ENFP.[35] Each letter represents a binary variable, and my combination boils down

---

35   Cancer sun, Sagittarius rising; Ravenclaw waxing, Hufflepuff waning.

to "an extroverted person with a lot of feelings who relies on instinct and perception rather than facts and good judgment." Everything after the word *extrovert* is pretty much a non-negotiable identification for me, and I wholeheartedly accept it. Extroversion made sense to me too, since I always enjoyed team sports (though, perhaps this was more about the well-documented homoeroticism of athletics and the butch gym teachers who stewarded them) and often found myself an outspoken group member and a natural-born, self-selected leader.

But I was explaining to Julie that being around people often left me exhausted; that I felt safer and more relaxed in the comfort of my own home than I did around a lot of people; that most of my life actually transpires in conversations in my own head and in my journals.

She said, with the certainty with which she delivers most blows to my self-understanding, that I was an introvert. "You know that, right? You've been expected to be an extrovert your whole life, but you're not."

I felt instantly lighter. I wouldn't be needing people. What a relief. And being an INFP would allow me to be in a category with folks like William Shakespeare, from literature, and Sybil Branson, from Downton Abbey. I felt clear-headed and spent several days refusing to spend time with people, providing a very rational reason for doing so. A few weeks later, when I packed up my car and drove to New York, I did so with an unprecedented level of self-assuredness. In all the major moves and changes I had made in my life, I had never been so unencumbered by anxiety. I felt safe knowing that when I arrived, I wouldn't have to go to orientations or campfire initiations—I could trap myself in my apartment and no one in the entire city of New York would know to look for me.

And that's exactly what I did. I signed up for classes and writing workshops, which satisfied my need to socialize but only required vulnerability from me in safe spurts. I wandered around the cobbled streets in the West Village, sometimes carrying a camera in the hopes that I might capture the freedom I felt.

I loved everything about my new life. I loved the way the neon sign of the Corner Bistro glowed against old, red bricks. I had just graduated from a Master of Public Policy program, which I had realized within the first two weeks of school was only adjacently related to what I needed to do with my life. But now I was free from social expectations, which had once included both a way of being and ideas about what I was meant to do with my time. I didn't need to explain to classmates that telling stories was my plan to make the world a better place; it closely followed that I allowed myself to feel that my existence in New York was enough to make the world a better place.

I was defining myself daily. A couple of tourists asked me to take their picture on an iPhone. "Take a step back," I told them, with the authority of Annie Leibovitz. When they looked at the result, they asked if I was a photographer. I would be that for the day: "Yes, yes I am." I'd never see them again.

I met an old man named Lou at a bar in the West Village called the Black Derby. Lou saw me drawing a cartoon and he asked if I was a cartoonist.

"Yes, yes I am." I would be that for the day. I did go in to have a drink with Lou from time to time, but he had been in a car accident and had memory loss, so he didn't remember that I was the cartoonist he had met. Neither he nor the tourists had ever asked for credentials from me. They just witnessed me, and I let them watch.

I told stories. I didn't tell people that, with my master's degree, I was supposed to be taking a more active stand against Donald Trump's presidency, and so I didn't feel shame about it. My stories were enough. I made people laugh, which I had missed; I cried less, which I didn't miss. I was basically reborn. Being away from Duke, fully free of the school for the first time in seven years, I remembered what it was like to wake up without a boulder of dread on my chest. Only once I was away from that place did I realize that I had woken up almost every day I went there wishing that I were dead. And now I didn't. Now I wanted to be alive.

I cooked, I worked, I met up with acquaintances, I talked to Maddie on the phone every other day. I made small talk with baristas, I emailed friends back home. I talked loudly, I dressed accordingly, I told stories.

Whoever I was, I thought I was pretty happy.

Because I was taking a storytelling class at the Magnet Theater, in K-Town, I could see any of their shows for free. Determined to make the most of it—but more realistically, having no plans to fill my evenings—I went to watch shows often. I didn't quite understand the rhythm of the theater. I didn't know then that Wednesday was the night that house teams performed, or that Thursday was for a monthly rotation of one-off shows. I didn't know that there was a certain amount of reliability to the weekly schedule, I just glanced down at my watch on weeknights and thought it seemed like a good time for a laugh.

Arriving at the theater one night, however, I realized that this show was not part of the regular scheduling. This was a sex-themed burlesque show.

I panicked. As someone who can't say the word *vibrator* out loud without laughing, I knew that publicly partaking in sexual intimacy was going to be a real challenge for me.

I could leave?

The thing, though, about having a fear of intimacy is that it simultaneously captures your curiosity with unrivaled force. Everything that scares us fascinates us with its power to mesmerize. Or perhaps that's the very thing that terrifies us—that we want to get dangerously close.

For many years—since I first visited my older sister in New York, the summer I turned twenty—I would walk by a store called the Pleasure Chest. Part of me thought, "You could just go in there, you know. You could buy something if you wanted." If I didn't erupt into a fit of the giggles, I would think to myself, "If I went in there and bought a vibrator, what would I even do with it?!" as if that wasn't perfectly self-explanatory.

It was this same dilemma that captivated me at the Magnet that night. I could stay; no one would know. I had moved to New York to finally start being the person I was without any of my social strictures. Maybe getting to be more comfortable talking about sex was something I needed to learn. Perhaps I was a burlesque dancer myself, just waiting to bloom.

And in the middle of deciding, the show started, which quickly clarified for me that I did not want to be sitting in that audience. But as one of seven or so audience members, I was as good as initiated. I would join a cult if it meant not disappointing someone.

"I can do this," I thought, as they passed around a bucket. Inside would go penance for twenty-first-century humans. We were to write sex secrets. In the spirit of doing this, I wrote down a secret, not to be repeated now. But when they later read mine out loud, I felt sure that everyone could sense my body tense in self-betrayal.

The host got up on stage and asked the audience if we were ready to get sexy. I was not. But, "I can do this," I thought, as I reminded myself that I would never see these people again.

As she performed an introductory dance that looked like a series of stretches I would do on the soccer field—though during which I would never have made such intense eye contact with other people—I distracted myself by wondering if I could ever be earnest enough to do a dance like this in front of people and if she herself was feeling any embarrassment. I wondered how you make that kind of person.

A mummy did a strip tease to the "Monster Mash," and it occurred to me that sexy could be fun, that maybe my brand of sexy was wrapping my face in gauze and moving jerkily from side to side.

Next, the host announced that we were going to be doing an "intimacy exercise." This would involve making uninterrupted eye contact with a fellow audience member for ninety seconds. "Ideally, this would be with a stranger," the host winked at us. Like I had a choice—I was alone.

So, a girl with a snaggle tooth and one slightly lazy eye turned from her two friends to stare deeply into my eyes. I told myself that I had to do this in earnest—that I would not laugh defensively or shrug off the task.

But when I stared into her eyes, I realized that I wasn't going to laugh. I was going to cry. It was like I was finally admitting that I wanted to be seen by someone. That avoiding rejection isn't the same as contentment.

"Oh," I realized. "I'm lonely. So unbelievably lonely."

With Julie's assessment echoing in my head, I had traipsed around the West Village under the impression that I was perfectly immune to feelings of loneliness. I decided that, as an introvert, I was better off without the burden of company. But I had deluded myself into thinking that I could exist untethered from everyone. It's true that each day was an opportunity to reinvent myself, but that did nothing to help me along in my actual ambition to discover the best version of myself, because I hadn't found the people who brought that out in me. But what did that mean about my need for people?

Loneliness is not a feeling to sit with. A major difference between being alone and being lonely is that the latter prompts a desperate need to change one's condition—a condition that implies a *telos*. Olivia Laing wrote an entire book about her experiences, and the experiences of several famed artists, navigating this titular *place* of loneliness—*The Lonely City*.

Throughout her book, she describes a deeply rooted lack, an "unmistakable lack," a desire to have what she does not have, a loneliness, "which agitates always in two directions, towards intimacy and away from threat." So, the telos is perhaps muddled—because how can the journey from insecurity to security, from unstable to stable, be anything but unidirectional?

That is the obvious challenge of the human struggle, though; we're biological accidents trying to make sense of everything we do through flawed logic and, for those of us less guided by reason, through stories.

This book has no doubt been one of many futile attempts to create a liberating identity narrative, but what has been the direction of this story? Where is my loneliness pointing me? And what terrors did I see when I looked in my partner's eyes at a sex-themed burlesque show?

## Option A: I was an introvert masquerading as an extrovert

I'll begin where Julie pointed me, as she is, simply put, never wrong. In nearly five years that I have known her she has boiled down my core issues into succinct—and sometimes, brutal—truths. When she told me that I was an introvert, it was so easy to believe. I spread the news that I would now be identifying as an INFP, and of the people who cared at all about this, which was admittedly few, almost everyone quickly agreed that INFP made sense. In most settings, I was fairly sociable but not exactly what you would call a joiner. This wasn't a major barrier to success in grad school, but when I was an undergrad at Duke, this meant pretending to believe that sleeping outside from January to March to watch one basketball game wasn't the stupidest thing I've ever seen humans do.

Both at school and at home, it was impressed upon me that being social was a matter of cultural capital. There isn't a single information session for an elite college that doesn't reinforce that the true return on your two-hundred-thousand-dollar investment is "the people you will meet here."

A couple of years ago, I was accidentally added to a "Kappa Forever" Facebook group—despite the fact that I was kappa kappa cut during the first round of sorority recruitment—and saw more job postings from my not-sisters than I had ever received from the career services center. Affiliation makes this tiny blue-green marble navigable.

And in some cases, more governable. In her book *Quiet*, Susan Cain quotes multiple Ivy League university presidents of the mid-twentieth century as having an unabashed preference for gregarious students, of the "healthy extrovert kind." In all my years of schooling, from kindergarten to eighteenth grade, that vocal participation was worth at least a half-grade bump and would likely connect you better with teachers to boot. This doesn't even account for extracurricular extroversion—for instance, being a student body president and all the rewards that come with it. Cain also makes the case that business schools and modern workplaces seek extroversion, even if it's coded in other candidate search terms. Simply put, our culture loves and rewards extroversion (think sports fandoms, reality television, debutante balls).

I was primed for those good old American values from a young age. Socializing was just a fundamental part of my parents' lives. My lively attendance at dinner parties was encouraged far more than reading quietly in my room. I'm still getting reprimanded for the unconventional way I socialize. As recently as one year ago, my mother sat on my bed in a most serious manner and told me that it was really quite rude to not say a proper hello to the Ronsons the night before. I had come home late one night, on East Coast time and ready for bed, to find that my parents had only just gotten the party started and fully expected me to join.

A proper hello, of course, being something more extensive than what I did, which was walk in, give a hearty greeting, and then offer my many apologies for the fact that it was past my bedtime. Silly me.

For my parents, and my mother in particular, the obligation to socialize trumps almost every individual need. It has, for that reason, always been challenging to understand myself without deriving a persona from those around me.

At best, this has been a neat party trick. I have learned how to be the best host and the best guest. I know how to sense a room's atmosphere and identify what needs to be said, when, and by whom. You *will* leave a dinner party at my apartment thinking, "Well, that was a grand time."

At worst, however, this has been a never-ending obligation on my part to stifle my own needs—and any related healthy boundaries—to fit a crowd. That ability to hear a room's social timbre as if it were being played loudly on my parents' lacquered black grand piano has perhaps caused too much noise. Catch me at the right moment and you may see my eyes whirring back and forth as they take in information and determine a proper course of action, knowing that if I should fail in this mission, life as I know it will be over.

In my natural disposition, I am much more introspective and solitary than I think my parents would have preferred. I spent a lot of time alone. When I was old enough to take the bus to middle school, I would do so with the same spunk as Matilda carrying books home from the library. In the afternoon, I would shut myself in a small guest room in my house and play video games. When forced to surface for family dinners, I struggled to comfortably communicate and quickly grew exhausted in the presence of others. I was fairly nerdy and obsessive over the things I found interesting—at that age, mostly just the television show *Gilmore Girls*.

But before I got edgy enough to binge watch Warner Brothers shows, I would take up various hobbies, which is how I ended up with multiple magic sets. I would sit in my room practicing sleight of hand, my stuffed animals rendered totally speechless by my finesse.

I was exactly the kind of kid that does *not* make the most of an elite education. I have three or four friends from Duke, and none of them have offered me lucrative jobs. I kept a journal in college, a bulky thing with a cover modeled after, of all things, a British Holy Bible. The first page, which I ripped out due to embarrassment, fearful as I often was to really hear my inner monologue, but left tucked in place, is an account of my first week at school. "How can people connect so quickly with people they don't have anything in common with yet?"

I remember that first week distinctly, desperately waiting for classes to start so that I could begin meeting people in a way that felt less overwhelming—ideally by engaging in some hearty philosophical debate. I spent a lot of time watching television from my bed, avoiding the camaraderie of a dorm common room, feeling relieved but very self-aware of how alone I was.

College is a particularly hard time for introverts, I would guess. I fared much better in graduate school, when people shared a lot more of my interests and viewed drinking and going out as a secondary priority. Still, I recognized in myself a tendency to hold my breath after a long day, meeting with one more project team and wanting to go eat alone at home. I made amazing friends for whom I have the utmost respect and affection, but spending time with people made me anxious as I tried to perform in a socially acceptable manner.

Months elapsed with a building sense of anguish before Julie would finally free me from my obligation to impress. But she might not have had all the information she really needed to make an accurate assessment.

Because in the evenings, when I would finally get back to binging television, the deep breath I took wasn't actually relief—it was release. I would burst into tears, craving intimacy and care. Leah would try to console me, but I didn't know how to explain what I was feeling, which was a profound and existential loneliness.

So how could I consider myself a pure introvert being *forced* into sociability?

## Option B: I was an extrovert cornered into introversion

Julie's word is holier to me than any god's, but maybe she was wrong, because damn it, I love people. I love talking to them, I love thinking about them, I love pretending to have conversations with them in my head, I love making them laugh.

As a preteen, I relied—perhaps too heavily—on the company of peers for reassurance, the absence of which would leave me feeling anxious. My first week of high school, I spent part of the too-long lunch block alone in the bathroom. Make no mistake, sitting alone is quite a different thing from hiding. And I was hiding—from that unbearable feeling of being visibly, and potentially contagiously, lonely.

Once I got to know people—or rather, once I let people get to know me—I passed time by being boisterous and disruptive. My eighth-grade report card said that I was sometimes more interested in making the class laugh than grasping math concepts.

It wasn't until high school, where most of our classes were taught in seminars, that I started to like school. You can imagine that I was exactly the kind of talkative blowhard receiving undue praise that Susan Cain warns against (in fact, at a house party, a popular boy named Julian told me that I talked a lot in class but that I was most certainly full of shit).

Recognizing this need to participate led me to sit in the very front row of my freshman year physics lecture at Duke. Two people knew my name on campus, but two hundred people knew me as the girl who sat in the front row and asked questions. I learned that this was extremely annoying to people.

In the same journal entry in which I decided that college wasn't a good fit for me, the desperation for company and meaningful relationships is obvious. I desperately wanted to be known.

It took me several lonesome months in New York to really understand that I don't actually prefer to spend my time alone; I'm even more certain that I don't want to *be* alone.

There is also, of course, the most confusing part of my so-called introversion: my love of performing.

When I locked myself in my childhood bedroom for hours on end, it was often so that I could use a single-player karaoke game on an old TV, shaped like a black pyramid that had fallen to one side. I faced the crowd of roughly drawn avatars who all bobbed with inhuman repetition and gave the best rendition of "Twist and Shout" I could muster. To this day, hearing the opening piano run on "I Will Survive" causes me to steel myself for a grand entrance. And I wasn't without flair, either—I knew how to give a crowd-pleasing rasp on a precisely chosen "hey." When opportunities allowed—at birthday parties or little league banquets—I took to the stage, feeling the confidence of a ten-thousand-hour expert.

At the end of high school, I passed my senior capstone project by performing a ten-minute stand-up set in front of my class. I kept doing stand-up and sketch comedy in college. I was best able to find myself in New York when I was telling stories in front of an audience. I've written a nearly two-hundred-page book sharing myself with you, my dozens of readers.

### Option C: We're not really talking about introversion and extroversion, are we?

I'm going to peer at you over my gold-rimmed librarian glasses and say with a smirk, "You already know the answer to that question." I'm a social introvert and an introspective extrovert. None of these words matter because we're really talking about something more like violent self-erasure, and clinging to either one of them is just an attempt to ground myself in something stabilizing. Because what we're all looking for is recognition and belonging.

Identity erasure is rampant for anyone who exists outside the mainstream. It was true for women whose contributions to art were overlooked, such as the wives of painters who kept their husbands from falling apart; it was especially true for black women written out of history and who are slowly having their stories uncovered. Katherine Johnson, for example, was a black woman working at NASA whose work as a mathematician was crucial to successfully sending humans into space.

In her book *In the Dream House*, Carmen Maria Machado, a Cuban-American queer woman, documents the invisibility of queer folks, who have always existed but have only recently been recognized as a people worthy of recognition. Today, bi erasure is an example of a current battleground; as lesbians like me rise to relative power (the illezminati, if you will), folks with more nuanced sexualities, such as bi- and pansexuality, have had to justify their identities to gays and straights alike who still want them pick a side already.[36]

Erasure sucks, but for a lot of young folks, erasure is the obvious lesser of two evils. Because when your options are to be a harmless nonentity or a menace to society, safety comes first. Instead, we turn persecution inward. In an essay on gay loneliness for Huffington Post's *Highline*, Michael Hobbes points out that the trauma of repeatedly pretending to be straight can result in a PTSD that is dull but resilient. Instead of an acute trauma, you have a deep-seated neurological reaction to certain activities. After correcting yourself hundreds of times for not acting like a girl, or for looking too closely at one, you get a pang of anxiety in your gut when you approach the thing that scared you, the thing you now want desperately.

Danger lay in both directions for me. I adored people, but the thing I loved was also the thing that hurt me. I was lying in my sister's bed one morning, surrounded by her friends, who made me feel likable, when one of them asked if I wanted to join the butch club. I said sure. Then, while they laughed, my sister, in a moment of sibling defensiveness, told me that it would mean I was a lesbian.

"Oh."

---

36  It is beyond the scope of this book—or perhaps it is the entire scope of this book—to make the argument that demanding the organization of humans into clear-cut categories is the work of the patriarchy. And if you've ever needed someone else to make a choice so that you no longer have to sit with the discomfort of nuance, then you were probably acting as an agent of the patriarchy. There is no unified strategy for destroying an oppressive system, but seeing each human as capable of infinities in their being, and resolutely fighting to know them, is a good place to start.

They were making fun of me, and my sister was protecting me by keeping me from getting my gay card too early. This was far more serious than when my sister wouldn't decode for me why "krabbs4life" was a bad AIM screen name. It was a beautiful but tragic moment. On the one hand, my sister was protecting me from embarrassment and offering me the fiercest of loyalties against high school royalty; on the other hand, her defensive kinship, which so rarely surfaced, was indicative of the severity of the situation. Being gay was simply not an option.

My latent gayness probably wasn't the catalyst for my shame. I grew up believing that to be superlative was my goal. But that kind of mastery—the kind that requires you to be the best, the most, or even the least, of something—merely enhances the value that we've placed on an ideal. The thing to master comes before the person trying to achieve it.

There were rules and strategies to being the best host, the best student, the best woman; and worth was estimated by how small you could make that variable distance between a virtue and your little dot of a person. Optimally, I would be a winner, but as a back-up plan, I'd just try and minimize my failures. But that kind of thinking simply results in an inventory of the self as a documentation of our wrongdoing. Karen Smith has huge pores, Gretchen Wieners has a weird hairline, and Regina George has man shoulders. We live in a culture of shame, wherein every misstep (or even every step, for that matter) builds a case for your worthlessness as a human.

The result is that we try to distance ourselves from the things we've been taught to hate. We mirror the social dynamic we know best. We try to split ourselves into two—separating the ideal self from, well, authenticity. We feed the parts of us that we *want* to prioritize. For anyone holding out hope that they might belong to the normative mainstream, that means investing more in superficialities, like material wealth and temporary solutions to old age and mortality, which will arrive for all of us, wrinkled and not-wrinkled folks alike.

Carl Jung wasn't a Buddhist, I assume, but he and Thích Nhất Hạnh both agree that the more we try to pretend that we're only the bright and shiny versions of ourselves, the more haunted we are by those shadow selves. Needing people is about as human an instinct as they come, but if socializing threatens the defensive barriers we've put around our vulnerable souls, then isolation feels safe.

So maybe I knew there was something different about the way I wanted to connect with people. I avoided letting people know that I needed that connection. I suppose the thing that I wanted to keep most secret was how lonely I was—and how much I longed for love. How much I actually felt things that I pretended I didn't. Having my mom's quick wit and my dad's analytical brain, my defenses were powerful.

I turned everything into a joke. Tina Fey taught me to turn my loneliness and inability to relate to my peers into a socially approved lifestyle. It was too scary to ask for help, to essentially admit that I was different, so I used humor—because if I could make people double over in laughter, they might not notice the fear and sadness that was radiating from my entire body.

But, like anything alive and breathing, my shadow self fought to be seen. At best, I got drunk and cried, and someone would hold me, because when the class clown cries, people notice.

At worst, I hurt myself.

I was in a lot of pain and couldn't explain it. I sometimes hoped that I could get sick so that I could finally explain why everything hurt, and I could ask for comfort without begging.

But begging for love and asking for attention seemed a little extreme.

So instead, I once gave myself a black eye.

I tapped my Old Spice deodorant stick—the same one that secured my membership into groups of popular jocks—against my cheek bone until my face was red. The next morning, I had a bruise under my right eye. I only remember one person asking about it. I was caught off guard, like I hadn't been expecting—hoping, even—for someone to ask, "What happened to you?"

I came up with an unconvincing explanation and shuffled off to English I.

There it is. That push/pull that Laing talks about. The push away from isolation toward connection, which then catches you in a limbo, since both things repel you. There is no stability in the extremes. Both isolation and connection have proved threatening to me at various times.

Imagine sitting on a swing and being pulled back in one direction. Upon release, you swing fast toward a point as far past center as you can get, and you rest for a second before feeling gravity pulling you backwards.

I spent most of my childhood making a home in isolation, so sure I was that my long pause there was permanent. But I'm really not sure I enjoyed being solitary.

Two years later, I acted again. In my bathroom, crying over nothing in particular, I took tiny scissors—the kind people use to make their eyebrows look good—and dragged them across my left wrist. I opened my eyes and found that even skin delicate enough to show tendons and veins wouldn't split if you didn't try hard enough to make it. I settled instead for scratching myself over and over so that the next morning, a cross-hatching of thin, red lines appeared below the heel of my hand.

Then I kept my hands tucked into my sleeves all day, so convinced that no one cared for me that I made it impossible for anyone to prove that they did. I wasn't ready to be fully vulnerable—to cut myself open and actually see blood.

That had long been my most tightly held secret. Because I didn't cut to swallow my pain—I cut to call my pain forward. As Leslie Jamison would put it, it was "affective downward mobility—cutting as a failure to feel better, as deliberately going on a kind of sympathetic welfare …" Yes. A pathetic cry for sympathy, when I felt that there was no way to ask for it. How often had I dreamed of obtaining an injury so that someone might help me carry something, *anything?* Immediately after the flashes of those fantasies, I would berate myself for wanting something so literally and figuratively sick.

And then Jamison affirms me: "Isn't wanting attention one of the most fundamental traits of being human—and isn't granting it one of the most important gifts we can ever give?" To see and be seen as we really are. Isn't that the whole point?

Of course, there was Maddie, who seemed to find nothing wrong with the fact that I wanted to fall asleep holding her. But one night she drunk kissed me and I withdrew faster than I could figure out if that was what I really wanted.

Then there was Paige, who consented to being the first great love of my life. Being kissed by a girl turned out to be exactly what I really wanted. Even when we broke up, I couldn't change what I knew, which was that I liked being intertwined with people.

And after we broke up—my heart a bruised, pulpy thing—I thought that flaunting my broken heart was better than hiding it away. But the swing had hardly come to a place of rest. I did what Andy Warhol once did, who, according to Laing, "made virtue of his vulnerability, and forestalled or neutralized possible taunts. Nobody could ever 'send him up.'" I've been vulnerable. I've also braced myself so fully for rejection and loneliness that I've actually knocked myself out of the running.

I have so proudly offered my damaged heart to the world that I sometimes forget to mention that I'm doing my best to heal, too.

And look how artfully I've pulled off my latest trapeze act. I've been perfectly honest with you, but being vulnerable with everyone isn't necessarily the same thing as being vulnerable with *someone*. I've written you this book so that I could tell you everything I needed you to know without having to sit across from you, where I would have hoped so desperately for you to hold my hands, and feared so greatly that you wouldn't that I would have kept them clenched on my lap. Isn't this one more affective performance of vulnerability? Like self-deprecating humor or a tearful "goodbye forever"?

Laing makes a lot out of windows in her book. There's a lot of looking out, peering in, hiding from, opening, and closing windows. Intimacy is that thing where you look out a window at the exact moment when someone looks in it. And you stare, and they stare, and no one looks away.

It's an easy bravery to stand and say, "These are my flaws, these are my faults, take me or leave me." It's something altogether harder to say, "These are my flaws, these are my faults, please take me, don't leave me."

So that's what I saw when I finally made eye contact with the girl with the snaggle tooth in the Magnet Theater. I saw someone looking at me, and I felt the terror and joy of being seen, of *watching* someone see me.

And I want that. More than anything in the world, I want that. Am I lonely?

I could tell you that I'm not. I could tell you how I go on dates with myself and how I make elaborate, one-plate brunches. I could tell you that I pour all the love I would give to a partner into my own self, and I answer to no one.

All that's true. I've figured out the way I want to dress, and I've cut my hair without wondering what my partner thinks, and I've bombed on stages with no witnesses.

But am I lonely? Yeah, I am. I am so *very* scared of being alone. My life is better shared. The point of this essay wasn't to prove that it's not. The point is that the swing has stopped. And it's here I wait.

# Epilogue

I MOVED TO LOS Angeles. I shaved my head. Am I a cliché representative of the ongoing queer freedom journey? Yeah. And that's okay. Better actually.

Cliché is a funny word—an attack on concepts that usually serve us pretty well. "I thought I knew what love was until I met you," "I would rather die than lose you," "I moved to Los Angeles and shaved my head." Someone else's jaded unhappiness casts a sense of naïveté over things we all kind of want. I mean, my sister would truly rather die than lose her hair, but the freedom to do what we want with our bodies without fearing retribution? I'd say that's a pretty fundamental desire. It's so easy to roll our eyes at these declarations, to label them as dramatic performances, but life is a drama and everything is a performance. It just so happens that some lifestyles are performed so consistently and in such large numbers that we lose our ability to see that they are clichés in themselves. If you find yourself in Madison Square Park in early summer, and you sit at a Shake Shack table, just outside the offices of New York's biggest banks, and you see groups of six or seven white twenty-year-olds in matching navy work pants and collared shirts that are a blue at or around the #cfecf7 what I mean.

The cliché is a pretty close cousin of the stereotype. Like most people in minority groups, I have spent my life navigating stereotypes[37]—first by rejecting them so adamantly that I actually wore skirts to our college bar, and then by chasing my own happiness and desires so desperately that I have wound up reinforcing some of those stereotypes. I'm, happily, the dykey lesbian that I always feared people would assume I was! And yet, even though I am incidentally following the exact pre-conceived path that loomed over my nineteen-year-old self, I feel *free*. And honestly, pretty fucking cool, too. And the less time I spend wondering whether people see me and see a big fat L on my person, the happier I am. The short hair, the sports bras, the letterman jackets. I don't feel like a lesbian—I feel like me.

---

[37] Melissa Harris-Perry's book *Sister Citizen: Shame, Stereotypes, and Black Women in America* has been fundamental in helping me understand how stereotypes work as a weapon for the powerful—that having to navigate around them, either by conforming to them or by contorting away from them, is exactly the violence that power structures enact against minorities.

## Fred

There are times when I look at myself in the mirror and I try to see hints of my story. I try to qualify my short hair as "my old hair, now shorter"—the hair I let friends straighten on big nights my sophomore year of high school, the hair that never cooperated, the hair whose very same tendency to stick straight up has actually made my short hair—or just, "my hair"—have impeccable waves rivaling those of Timothée Chalamet.

Sometimes, I see it. I see my resolve to be someone different that eventually gave out. Because, if it wasn't clear throughout these pages, there was nothing I wanted more or would have made greater sacrifices for than my desire to belong somewhere. Sometimes, I feel like I am "going through a phase." Not like, with my sexuality, obviously, but with the hair and the hats and the boxers and the ties and the skateboard. I wonder if, as my mom continues to suggest, I might want to wear a dress again someday. I wonder if my more masculine presentation is more performative than personal. Like anyone who spends most of their life pretending, I wonder if this is more dress-up.

Or determination. Or stubbornness. Or defiance. And that's the issue, I think. People like me, and people who have different experiences as marginalized people navigating a mainstream world, are trapped wondering whether we are being our true authentic selves. Leslie Jamison wrote all about women (probably cisgender in this context) having wounds and *being* wounds— women who are ailing attachments to men, who need to be supported by their stronger man (again, probably cisgender), and, I guess, by the patriarchy in general. A more traditional worldview, in which women are the weaker sex, requires that women remain meek, complacent, *un*-determined, *un*-stubborn, *un*-defiant. Because if they don't, they might find themselves working in politics and being called a nasty woman, or, more recently for Rep. Alexandria Ocasio Cortez, a "f-ing bitch." I've been called "bossy," like Tina Fey, and "shrill" like Lindy West, or "whiny," like most women making a well-reasoned argument for feminism.

And if you're not a cis, white woman, well, then there's a whole different sort of hell waiting for you if you act up; though more appropriately we may call this "acting out"—out of our social predeterminations, and into something that approaches true authenticity.

As transgender rights activist Janet Mock wrote about selecting her own name: "There's power in naming yourself, in proclaiming to the world that this is who you are."

A heteronormative world would have it that you suffer from an inability to name yourself for what feels true; in attempting to silence the joys of discovering your own understanding of gender, sexuality, and identity, fearful oppressors might be able to label you as weak, for failing to conform to someone else's definitions, rather than as victorious, for discovering your own.

I hurt for a long time. I hurt in places I didn't even know lived inside of me. I hurt facing one direction and I hurt facing the other, confronting either the world's cruelty or my own—for, in the times when the world didn't seem to hate me because I fit better, I hated myself for betraying who I really am.

Truthfully, the world doesn't want us to be unique. History does, but you have to live first in order to die. Boxes and categories are shortcuts for humans to process what's around them. They help us "understand" and move on. But each of us has the distinct opportunity to shatter the worlds of those around us by being individuals; most of us, for good reason, choose not to do so.

Some of us are so profoundly "confusing," that we're bulls in china shops, shattering away, even with the lightest step.

And sometimes, when I look in that mirror, I see a bull and I see the china I've broken. I see the fights I had to have to justify my clothing, I see the uproar around cutting my hair, I see the perfect daughter I could have been.

Julie (my therapist—if you don't know that by now, then I just don't know what else I could do to canonize her) and I joked recently that the sick irony of my life was that my greatest drive was to belong at all costs—a desire that couldn't be more tested by my queer body if I tried. My gender identity, which refuses to align with woman, man, and sometimes even non-binary, is so "mysterious" that many people don't have the language to understand it. And all I want is to have people see me clearly for who I am.

Then I see it in another way. I see my dad bringing home that Spider-Man suit or buying me that skateboard with a spacescape on the bottom, and I see my Pop giving me my pocket knife in the front seat of his green truck. I see myself running around shirtless in Jeff Larson's basement, thumping at my chest, because I wasn't old enough to *have* boobs, let alone think of them as such. I see Robin Hood and John Deeres and, of course, I see Fred. The plate-licking, genderless camper who named herself, even in the absence of any prompting to do so. And I wonder if Fred has just been waiting to join me in my real life and if I've finally decided to make room to let them.

# Artist Thanks

THIS BOOK WOULD be nothing without the assistance of these artists, who turned my book from messy manuscript to final print run. Let it never be assumed that a writer works alone. It can be solitary work, but in my experience, the following collaborators were crucial to the completion of this book, even if it is my name on the cover.

# Kit Haggard
*Developmental Editor, Copyeditor*

KIT HAGGARD'S FICTION HAS appeared in *The Kenyon Review, Prairie Schooner, Electric Literature,* and *The Masters Review,* among other places; critical essays on queer literature and fabulism have appeared in a number of outlets. She is the recipient of the St. Botolph Emerging Artists Award, the Rex Warner Prize, and the Nancy Lynn Schwartz Prize for Fiction. Haggard is a full-time editor and writer, and lives in Boston with her spouse and many, many houseplants. More of her work can be found at kithaggard.work

# Sarah Perry

*Developmental Editor*

SARAH PERRY IS THE author of the memoir *After the Eclipse*, which was named a New York Times Book Review Editors' Choice, a Poets & Writers Notable Nonfiction Debut, and a Barnes and Noble Discover Great New Writers pick. Perry is the recipient of a 2020-2022 Tulsa Artist Fellowship, the 2018 Betty Berzon Emerging Writer Award, and

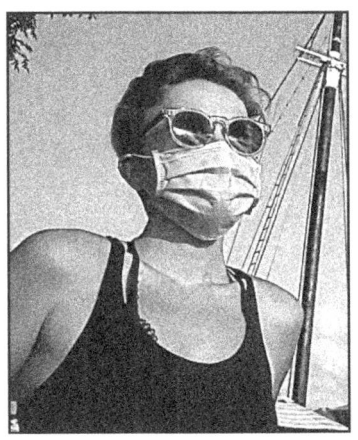

*Photo credit: Donna Ferrato*

fellowships from the Edward F. Albee Foundation, VCCA, Playa, and The Studios of Key West. She holds an M.F.A. in nonfiction from Columbia University.

Perry will be Assistant Professor of Creative Writing at the University of North Texas beginning in fall 2022. She was the 2019 McGee Distinguished Professor of Creative Writing at Davidson College, and has also taught at Columbia University, Manhattanville College, The Sackett Street Writers' Workshop, the Unterberg Poetry Center at the 92nd Street Y, and Catapult. Her writing has appeared in Off Assignment, Elle magazine, The Guardian, and other outlets.

Originally from Maine, Perry spent ten years in the Southeast and ten years in Brooklyn, New York. She currently lives in Tulsa, Oklahoma, where she is working on two books: a sequel memoir titled *The Book of Regrets* and a collection of one hundred short essays called *Sweet Nothings*

# Anna Alcaro

*Illustrator*

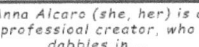
Anna Alcaro (she, her) is a professional creator, who dabbles in ...

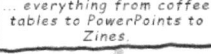
... everything from coffee tables to PowerPoints to Zines.

She began her illustrating career selling drawings to her classmates in the 2nd grade while growing up in Western Pennsylvania.

During her artistic journey, she's set out to act on her innate impulse to create rather than explicitly honing one craft or another. This has manifested in ...

graphic facilitating at her day job,

selling commissioned illustrations to friends and strangers to give as holiday gifts,

and winning art contests, as she did with a series called Vices: Dictators Eating Ice Cream (2014).

She plans to continue to put art and created objects into the world for the next 50-70 years.

When she isn't creating or working full time, she is making beautiful meals

going to concerts,

or hosting a faith based LGBTQIA+ group through the Table Church DC, to support friends as they collectively process their intersecting identities.

Anna lives in Washington DC with her partner and their two dozen house plants.

You can follow her on Instagram @annaalcaro.

# Colleen Sheehan

*Literal godsend, designer,
production manager*

COLLEEN SHEEHAN BECAME a book design critic at seven and started designing books at twenty-six. That's nineteen years of obsessing about type. There's just something about how those letters fit together that caught her attention and hasn't relinquished its entrancing hold yet.

Colleen hasn't won any awards because she hasn't submitted to any. She hasn't been a guest speaker at a major university or design conference, has no more than 1,500 followers across all social media channels, and nobody has ever approached her on the street and known who she was. The only ones who do are the two hundred and sixty-plus authors and publishers who have had a book designed by them. And really, that's about all the recognition she can handle.

## Annie Krabbenschmidt

She's been queer her whole life and now identifies as a toadish hermit gremlin. Colleen lives in Ames, IA with her exquisitely brilliant, gorgeous, genius author wife of sixteen years, a weiner dog who will wear only shirts with no pants, and an ancient orange tabby who enjoys feasting on animals 500 times his size from tiny cans provided by capitalism.

*FRED* is approximately book 664 that she's designed since 2014 and may be the most relevant book to her own experiences she's ever done.

# Works Consulted

Adam, Hajo, and Adam D. Galinsky. "Enclothed Cognition." *Journal of Experimental Social Psychology*, vol. 48, no. 4, 2012, pp. 918–25. *Crossref*, www.sciencedirect.com/science/article/abs/pii/S0022103112000200.

Baldwin, James. *The Fire Next Time*. First Vintage International Edition, Vintage, 1993.

Chbosky, Stephen. *The Perks of Being a Wallflower*. MTV Books/Gallery Books, New York, Gallery Books, 2012.

Gay, Roxane. *Bad Feminist: Essays*. New York, Harper Perennial, 2014.

---. *Hunger: A Memoir of (My) Body*. New York, HarperCollins, 2017.

Gregory, Alice. "Lessons from the Last Swiss Finishing School." *The New Yorker*, 1 Oct. 2018, www.newyorker.com/magazine/2018/10/08/lessons-from-the-last-swiss-finishing-school.

Hanh, Thich Nhat. *You Are Here: Discovering the Magic of the Present Moment*. English Translation, Boulder, Shambhala, 2009.

Hobbes, Michael. "Everything You Know About Obesity Is Wrong." *The Huffington Post*, 19 Sept. 2018, highline.huffingtonpost.com/articles/en/everything-you-know-about-obesity-is-wrong.

## Annie Krabbenschmidt

---. "The Epidemic of Gay Loneliness." *The Huffington Post*, 1 Mar. 2017, highline.huffingtonpost.com/articles/en/gay-loneliness.

Jamison, Leslie. *The Empathy Exams: Essays.* 1st ed., Minneapolis, Graywolf Press, 2014.

Kornhaber, Spencer. "'Boy Erased' and the Rise of Queer Coming-of-Age Films." *The Atlantic*, 15 Nov. 2018, www.theatlantic.com/magazine/archive/2018/12/the-queer-coming-of-age-movie-arrives/573925.

Laing, Olivia. *The Lonely City.* New York, Picador, 2016.

Machado, Carmen Maria. *In the Dream House.* Minneapolis, Graywolf Press, 2019.

Rilke, Rainer Maria, and Stephen Mitchell. *Letters to a Young Poet.* First Vintage Books Edition, New York, Vintage, 1986.

Rudman, Laurie A., and Peter Glick. *The Social Psychology of Gender, Second Edition: How Power and Intimacy Shape Gender Relations.* New York, The Guilford Press, 2008.

Solnit, Rebecca. *Men Explain Things to Me.* Chicago, Haymarket Books, 2014.

Tolentino, Jia. "Always Be Optimizing." *Trick Mirror*, New York, Random House, 2019, pp. 63–94.

Wiman, Christian. *Ambition and Survival: Becoming a Poet.* Port Townsend, Copper Canyon Press, 2007.

# Acknowledgements

AT THE END of this long journey, my gratitudes will have to be a lot more condensed than I once hoped they'd be. This is partly due to the fact I am tired, and partly due to the fact that I don't have a proofreader for this section.

Regardless, my first and most important thanks go to Miranda Rosenblum, for their generosity, patience, and kindness. Miranda was the first person to help me understand my gender identity, even while they were advocating for their own. They have taught us all with empathy and understanding, asking for nothing even though they deserve everything. Friend, you saved my life in more ways than one. This book wouldn't exist without your encouragement, support, reading, thoughtfulness, and wisdom. If I could have dedicated this book to you without offending my family I would have.

To Sarah Perry, Kit Haggard, and Leah Ling, your feedback and edits made this a much better book than it would have been without you. Even though I pretty much rewrote this entire book with your notes, I'm glad I did because I finally saw my story written as I always thought it could be.

## Annie Krabbenschmidt

Colleen Sheehan, my lord am I lucky to have found you. From your genius as a designer, to your emotional support as I try to publish, I'm so grateful to you for making me laugh with every Zoom meeting password you make.

Anna Alcaro, thank you for taking on this project and giving it so much more life than words alone could offer. I'm glad to call you a friend and colleague.

Thank you to everyone who pre-ordered the book and gave me a reason to finish this project. Thank you especially to Peter and Erik Jensen, MR Courtney Benham, Adam Hollowell, James Moore, Michael Parks, and Leah Ling, for your generous contributions. To RQDP founding members—the Mullen-Matthews family and the Flynn family—thank you so much for believing in this project.

To the Branson community at large, thank you for caring for me and giving me a place to call home during the day. To all my classmates, teammates, captains, coaches, and teachers, thank you for helping me understand myself. Ms. Moore was the first person to make me feel like a decent writer, and though I will probably need years of constant reassurance, her subtle encouragements have stuck with me. All-in-all, Branson will always be an extremely special place for me, and it gave me the best education—spiritually, emotionally, and academically—that I could have asked for. I'm not sure I even know where my college degree is, but I have every material good that reminds me of high school immortalized in my childhood bedroom.

Mr. Henrikson, you are a most important mentor to me. To have your friendship, a decade and a half after stepping foot in your freshman history class, means the world to me. You have always been an exemplar of true wisdom, and your opinions on anything, from my love life to my career, are worth more than their weight in gold.

Duke failed me in so many ways, but I will forever be grateful for the people in my life that came to me from my time there. Weirdly enough, I have had the extreme pleasure of getting to know way more Duke alumni since I graduated, many of whom are truly the coolest, smartest, most interesting people I've ever met.

To DWCS, I love you now more than ever. Through the greatest of tragedies in losing Sophie, I am reminded that this team was a family to me and many others since the day I joined. To one of you in particular, Robin, thank you for all you did. Thanks for making me do, well, everything, from coming out to camping in a rainstorm. I love you. I don't say it enough, but I do.

I'm also grateful for my two favorite professors.[38] Nick, when I walked to your lectern in the first month of school, I was holding back tears. In an hour, you somehow had me convinced that I not only had a place in the MPP program, but also that it was an important one. You were one of the first professors to make me feel like I had intellectual contributions to make. You've been helping me write this book since that first meeting. Thanks for your friendship as I keep working on my research.

Oh Adam. What a journey we've had together. Within a moment of your introductions to Ethics in an Unjust World, I knew you were a teacher I needed to learn from. I might have secretly hoped that we would become friends, but I never could

---

38  Three if you include Frau Freytag. She didn't help me with this book, but BOY is that woman a hoot.

have imagined a more wonderful journey for us. At the start of our friendship, I told you that the only thing I knew about my career was that I wanted "to be asked to teach, to be asked to speak, and to be asked to write." Even though you made fun of me for wanting to be "asked," you gave me an opportunity to do all three by the time I graduated from Sanford and I am extremely aware of the poetic beauty in that. Thank you for every book you gave me, one of which contained a note about lifting my voice—a note that sits framed on my desk. Thank you for your empathy, humor, and carefully considered optimism. I'm grateful to call you a friend.

To all the friends who read pieces of this book—from early readers, like Katie Jane and Christine, to the generous souls who read whenever I sent out a panicked plea, like Miranda, Maddie, Kelly, and Macy—your generosity in reading leaves me humbled beyond words.

Thanks to Catapult, I had more readers and teachers and editors than I bargained for, all of whom made this book better. Zaina, Haley, Sarah, and Elissa, I think you're the coolest, smartest people ever and some of the best teachers I've ever had, and through your example, I got to work with my very talented classmates, who made my work better.

To the Freeman Street writing group—Sunny, Rachel, Vesna, and Mary—you changed my life by welcoming me into a writing group well before I considered myself a writer. You challenged me, you encouraged me, you cheered for me. I couldn't have asked for a better source of wisdom as I started this project.

To everyone at the Magnet Theater, thank you for giving me the confidence to put myself out there. Adam Wade, I'm so grateful to you for your encouragements. I started your class shaky and full of self-doubt, and I emerged a very confident storyteller. That's some teacher.

To everyone who has ever attended a show, read a piece, laugh reacted to an Instagram story, every iota of support I have received from my friends and family helped me to carry on when I wanted to give up. Thank you for engaging with me and challenging me when necessary.

I owe a great deal of gratitude to all the found families I have in my world, for their support in this book and in my life. Sometimes I get socially anxious, but your friendships are so important to me. From the leap day dinner guests, to the five-borough beer and bike tour, to a teary trip to the Poconos, to a fireside reading of Jane Austen, to a water balloon toss on the first day of school, to the gayborhood watch, to a very famous podcast, to the Breck family band, to a childhood of yellow vs. pink, to my brother-roommates, to my elephant shoes. I don't always know how to show it, but I'm at home when I'm with you. Thanks to you, I knew how to identify love when I found it.

Which of course brings me to my best friend, Al. I'm learning what a great partnership is from being with you. No one makes me laugh as hard, no one inspires me more, and no one makes me feel more loved and supported every second of the day. I love you so much.

Jackie, I'm really glad you've adopted yourself into our family. It really wouldn't be the same to travel the world without you. I'm so proud of you and the life you made for yourself. Thank you for opening your New York apartment to me that summer, it changed my life.

## Annie Krabbenschmidt

Catherine, thanks for teaching me to read at four so I could write a story that made a teacher laugh at seven. I think you're one of the most brilliant people on the planet—I don't even think you realize the size shoes I had to fill as I went from grade to grade, but they were far larger than a women's six. There isn't a thing in this world you couldn't do if you put your mind to it. Plus, and it kills me to admit this in my very own book, but you're unmatched in your humor and wit. Thank you for taking midnight calls, threatening my enemies, editing resumes, researching accessories, and being my best friend growing up.

Dad, I am in awe at how you much you're willing to learn about the world and rethink your stances on anything from the economy to gender. Without a doubt I know I got the problem-solving side of my brain from you, and this book and career has just been one big weird puzzle that I'm proud to say I got through, but only with your support.

Mom, I hope you know how wonderful I think you are. I know that sometimes it stresses you out to see me absolutely disregard everything you taught me about wearing a hat inside, but I know that you've been my biggest supporter since day one. Everything I try to be is because of who you are.

# About the Author

ANNIE KRABBENSCHMIDT (she/they) is a writer with too many hobbies. Her writing has appeared almost nowhere else, and she certainly has never been paid for it. They live in Los Angeles with two beautiful grown men roommates, and a pittie mix named Tobin Heath. Annie is happily partnered—sorry to disappoint.

CPSIA information can be obtained
at www.ICGtesting.com
Printed in the USA
JSHW022244270522
26334JS00003B/210